LEARNING ADVENTURES IN SCIENCE

Grades 5–6

By the Staff of Score@Kaplan

Foreword by Alan Tripp

Simon & Schuster

**This series is dedicated to our
Score@Kaplan parents and children—
thank you for making these books possible.**

Published by
Kaplan Educational Centers and Simon & Schuster
1230 Avenue of the Americas
New York, NY 10020

Special thanks to: Elissa Grayer, Doreen Beauregard, Julie Schmidt, Rebecca Geller Schwartz, Linda Lott, Janet Cassidy, Marlene Greil, Nancy McDonald, Sarah Jane Bryan, Chris Wilsdon, Janet Montal, Jeannette Sanderson, David Stienecker, Dan Greenberg, Kathy Wilmore, Dorrie Berkowitz, Brent Gallenberger, and Molly Walsh

Head Coach and General Manager, Score@Kaplan: Alan Tripp
President, Score@Kaplan: Robert L. Waldron
Series Content and Development: Mega-Books
Project Editor: Mary Pearce
Production Editor: Donna Mackay, Graphic Circle Inc.
Art Director: Elana Goren-Totino
Illustrators: Rick Brown, Ryan Brown, Sandy Forrest, Larry Nolte, Evan Polenghi, Fred Schrier, Peter Spacek, Arnie Ten
Cover Design: Cheung Tai
Cover Photograph: Michael Britto

Manufactured in the United States of America
Published Simultaneously in Canada

January 1998
10 9 8 7 6 5 4 3 2 1

ISBN:0-684-84435-4

Contents

Grade Five

Grade Six

Dear Parents,

Your child's success in school is important to you, and at Score@Kaplan we are always pleased when the kids who attend our educational centers do well on their report cards. But what we really want for our kids is not just good grades. We also want everything that good grades are supposed to represent:

- We want our kids to master the key communication systems that make civilization possible: language (spoken and written), math, the visual arts, and music.
- We want them to build their critical-thinking skills so they can understand, appreciate, and improve their world.
- We want them to continually increase their knowledge and to value learning as the key to a happy, successful life.
- We want them to always do their best, to persist when challenged, to be a force for good, and to help others whenever they can.

These are ambitious goals, but our children deserve no less. We at Score@Kaplan have already helped thousands of children across the country in our centers, and we hope this series of books for children in first through sixth grades will reach many more households.

Simple Principles

We owe the remarkable success of Score@Kaplan to a few simple principles. This book was developed with these principles in mind.

- We expect every child to succeed.
- We make it possible for every child to succeed.
- We reinforce every instance of success, no matter how small.

Assessing Your Child

One helpful approach in assessing your child's skills is to ask yourself the following questions.

- How much is my child reading? At what level of difficulty?
- Has my child mastered appropriate language arts skills, such as spelling, grammar, and syntax?
- Does my child have the ability to express appropriately complex thoughts when speaking or writing?
- Does my child demonstrate mastery of all age-appropriate math skills, such as mastery of addition and subtraction facts, multiplication tables, division rules, and so on?

These questions are a good starting place and may give you new insights into your child's academic situation.

What's Going on at School

Parents will always need to monitor the situation at school and take responsibility for their child's learning. You should find out what your child should be learning at each grade level and match that against what your child actually learns.

The activity pages in *Learning Adventures* were developed using the standards developed by the professional teachers associations. As your child explores the activities in *Learning Adventures*, you might find that a particular concept hasn't been taught in school or hasn't yet been mastered by your child. This presents a great opportunity for both of you. Together you can learn something new.

Encouraging Your Child to Learn at Home

This book is full of fun learning activities you can do with your child to build understanding of key concepts in language arts, math, and science. Most activities are designed for your child to do independently. But, that doesn't mean that you can't work on them together or invite your child to share the work with you. As you help your child learn, please bear in mind the following observations drawn from experience in our centers:

- Positive reinforcement is the key. Try to maintain a ratio of at least five positive remarks to every negative one.
- All praise must be genuine. Try praises such as: "That was a good try," "You got this part of it right," or "I'm proud of you for doing your best, even though it was hard."
- When a child gets stuck, giving the answer is often not the most efficient way to help. Ask open-ended questions, or rephrase the problem.
- Remember to be patient and supportive. Children need to learn that hard work pays off.

There's More to Life Than Academic Learning

Most parents recognize that academic excellence is just one of the many things they would like to ensure for their children. At Score@Kaplan, we are committed to developing the whole child. These books are designed to emphasize academic skills and critical thinking, as well as provide an opportunity for positive reinforcement and encouragement from you, the parent.

We wish you a successful and rewarding experience as you and your child embark upon this learning adventure together.

Alan Tripp
General Manager
Score@Kaplan

Dear Kids,

Get your pencils sharpened, and put your game face on! You're about to begin a Learning Adventure. This book is filled with puzzles, games, riddles, and lots of other fun stuff. You can do them alone or with your family and friends. While you're at it, you'll exercise your brain.

If you get stuck on something, look for the Score coaches. Think of them as your personal brain trainers. You can also check your answers on pages 65–70, if you really have to.

We know you'll do a great job. That's why we have a special puzzle inside. After you do three or four pages, you'll see a puzzle piece. Cut it out, then glue it or tape it in place on page 64. When the puzzle is finished, you'll discover a hidden message from us.

So, pump up your mind muscles, and get ready to Score. You'll have a blast and boost your brain power at the same time.

Go for it!

Your Coaches at Score

A Toothy Tale

...see claims like this one:

...ntists recommend Sparko Toothpaste.

...ns always as true as they seem? Let's collect

...ad what some dentists say about Sparko.

...llow the directions below.

Dentist 1:	**Dentist 2:**	**Dentist 3:**	**Dentist 4:**	**Dentist 5:**
Sure, I recommend Sparko. My partner and I recommend all major toothpastes. Why not Sparko, too?	*All toothpastes are the same. Sparko is as good as any. That's how all 3 of the dentists in my office feel.*	*Sparko? The stuff with sparkles? The other 2 dentists in my office and I recommend it and others.*	*Toothpaste should be toothpaste. Sparko looks and tastes like candy. I don't recommend it.*	*Sparko is the best! Not because it works better, but because they give me FREE comic books for all my patients!*

Now make a graph of the data. Color in a box for each dentist who fits the category. Then write the answers to the questions.

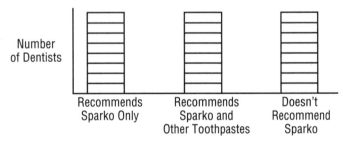

1. Did 9 out of 10 dentists really recommend Sparko? Explain. _____

_____

2. Of those who recommended Sparko, how many thought it was better than other toothpastes? _____

3. How many dentists didn't recommend Sparko? What were their reasons?_____

_____

_____

Conclusion: Would the claim that 9 of 10 dentists recommend it make you more likely to buy it? Why or why not?_____

NAME _____

Hoop Dreams

You can use graphs and tables to understand scientific relationships. Look at the tables and the graphs on these two pages. Put the information from the tables into graph form. Then answer the questions.

Possible Relationship: Tall basketball players score more points.

Name	Height	Points Scored per Game
Barb	4 ft. 9 in.	6.5
Phil	5 ft. 3 in.	14.0
Mookie	5 ft. 2 in.	11.2
Cheryl	5 ft. 6 in.	24.6

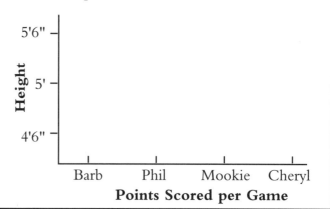

1. Do tall basketball players score more points? _____
   How would you describe the relationship between height and scoring points? _____

2. How many points per game would you expect a 6-foot player to score? _____

Possible Relationship: Basketball players with expensive sneakers score more points.

Name	Cost of Sneakers	Points Scored per Game
Barb	$ 39.95	6.5
Phil	$119.95	14.0
Mookie	$ 24.95	11.2
Cheryl	$ 87.50	24.6

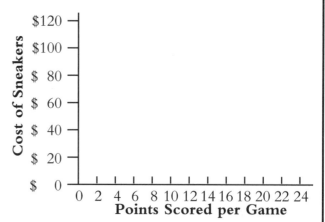

2

NAME

3. Do players with expensive sneakers score more points?_____
Explain your thinking. _____
_____

4. How would you describe the relationship between the cost of sneakers and scoring points?_____
_____

5. How many points per game would you expect a player with $239 shoes to score?_____ A player with $19.95 shoes?_____

Possible Relationship: Basketball players who practice more score more points.

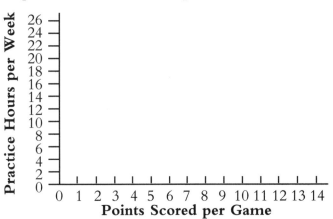

Name	Practice Hours per Week	Points Scored per Game
Jeff	3.5	7.0
Karla	13.5	26.0
Alison	6.5	11.0
Dov	7.5	15.0

6. Does practice help a player score more points? Explain your thinking. _____
_____

7. About how many points would a player who practiced 11.4 hours per week average? Explain how you got your answer.
_____
_____

A *relationship* is a connection between two or more things. Does one thing cause another? Does one thing affect another? When you find answers to these questions, you're discovering relationships.

NAME _____

Toast Table

Scientists sometimes use tables with rows and columns to present information. For example, suppose you needed a recipe for that old favorite, Burnt Toast. You could use a table like this one. Read the table, and then answer the questions.

Question: Why is a table like a pair of eyeglasses?

Because it helps you see your data better.

Favorite Burnt Toast Recipes				
Recipe	**Basic Burnt Toast**	**Burnt Toast Carbonara**	**Scorchies**	**Midnight Muffins**
Ingredients	1 slice bread	1 slice Italian bread	16 bread balls	muffin
Directions	Toast until charred and black.	Toast until black smoke comes out.	Cook in oven until scorched.	Toast until ruined.
Cooking Time	22 minutes	24 minutes, or until black	1 hour	1 hour, 8 minutes

WARNING: Do not try these recipes without parental supervision!

1. Which burnt toast recipe would you use if:
   a. You were in a hurry? _____
   b. You were having toast with spaghetti?_____
   c. You were having a party? _____
   d. You were having brunch? _____
2. How much longer do Scorchies take to make than Burnt Toast Carbonara? _____
3. Compare making 3 batches of Basic Burnt Toast, one after another, and making 1 batch of Midnight Muffins. Which would take longer? How much longer? _____

Now it's your turn to make your own table. Think of information that would be useful in table form. Then, on another piece of paper, make a table to present the information. Topics may include:

- Recipes for your favorite foods
- Ratings for your favorite movies
- Sports scores and information
- Your daily schedule

NAME_____

Experiment Expert

Are you an experiment expert? Circle the letter next to the words that complete each definition. Then follow the directions below.

1. A *hypothesis*
   a. is a side of a triangle.
   b. is a sports car that was popular during the '80s.
   c. is a statement you can test that could be either true or false.

2. An *experiment*
   a. is something that only scientists wearing lab coats can do.
   b. involves mixing up chemicals that may explode at any time.
   c. is a way to prove whether a hypothesis is true or false.

Read each hypothesis below. Then describe an experiment you could do to see if it is true. The first one is done for you.

Hypothesis: It is faster to take the bus to school than to walk.
Experiment: Try going to school both ways. Record the time it takes.

Compare the time._____

Hypothesis: Hot water freezes faster than cold water.
Experiment: _____

_____

Hypothesis: Plants grow better when they listen to music.
Experiment: _____

_____

Hypothesis: Eating junk food makes you "hyper."
Experiment: _____

_____

Write your own hypothesis on another sheet of paper. Then describe an experiment that would test it.

> A *hypothesis* is a statement you can test that could be either true or false. An *experiment* is a way to test whether a hypothesis is true or false.

NAME _____

Bye, Bye, Bubbles

Cola drinkers were in an uproar last week because their soda was flat. You are called in to investigate.

You may want to reread the definitions of hypothesis and experiment on page 5.

Bubble-Rageous Cola Drinkers Protest Flat Soda!
Dateline, March 9: Drinkers of the popular soft drink Bubble-Rageous Cola had a big surprise last week. Their soda was flat! Company spokesperson Valerie Vong announced a million-dollar investigation of the incident that will be performed by the well-known investigation firm of You & You.

Memo
From: Valerie Vong, Spokesperson for Bubble-Rageous Cola
To: You, head of the investigation firm, You & You
Regarding: Million-Dollar Flat Soda Investigation
As indicated earlier, we think this is what happened: The bottles were left open. For some reason, they were unusually warm. Does warm soda go flat faster than cold soda? This is the question we want you to answer.

Plan and perform an experiment that answers the question: Does warm soda go flat faster than cold soda? Use the following outline to get you started.

Your Hypothesis: _____

_____

Materials You Will Need: _____

_____

Your Plan:

Step 1 _____

Step 2 _____

Step 3 _____

On another piece of paper, record your thinking and data.

NAME_____

Now that you have the results of your experiment, read on to find out how Bubble-Rageous wants you to present the results. Follow the directions below.

> **Memo**
> **From:** Valerie Vong, Bubble-Rageous Cola Spokesperson
> **To:** You, head of the investigation firm, You & You
> **Regarding:** Results of Million-Dollar Flat Soda Investigation
> *As we agreed, you will now send us the results of your experiment begun on page 6, testing to see whether warm soda goes flat faster than cold soda. We would like to get your results in the following form:*

Hypothesis: Repeat your hypothesis here (see page 6). _____
_____

Procedure: In step-by-step order, explain what you did, and why you did it. _____
_____
_____

Results: On another piece of paper, present your data from page 6 in the form of one or more graphs and/or tables.

Analysis: Answer the following questions.

1. Did the results of your experiment support your hypothesis? Explain. _____
_____

2. Why do you think the Bubble-Rageous Cola went flat so fast?_____
_____

3. To make soda, gas is dissolved in liquid. When the gas escapes from the liquid, the soda goes flat. How can you use these statements to explain what happened in your experiment?_____
_____

4. Which would you expect to go flat faster — a glass of soda at 100°F or a glass of soda at 33°F? Explain. _____

NAME _____

Is it Alive?

Is a candle flame alive? How can you tell? Read about the common characteristics that living things share. Then read each item below. Put a check next to each word or phrase that correctly completes each sentence.

The Five Characteristics of Living Things

Energy: A living thing can get and use energy from its environment.

Response: A living thing can respond to changes in its environment.

Growth: A living thing can change its size and form.

Reproduction: A living thing can make similar copies of itself.

Cells: Living things are made of cells.

Cut out the puzzle piece. Glue or tape it in place on page 64.

1. A car
____ gets and uses energy.
____ responds to environmental changes.
____ grows.
____ reproduces.
____ is made of cells.
____ is a living thing.

2. A flame
____ gets and uses energy.
____ responds to environmental changes.
____ grows.
reproduces.
____ is made of cells.
____ is a living thing.

3. Bread mold
____ gets and uses energy.
____ responds to environmental changes.
____ grows.
____ reproduces.
____ is made of cells.
____ is a living thing.

4. A light bulb
____ gets and uses energy.
____ responds to environmental changes.
____ grows.
____ reproduces.
____ is made of cells.
____ is a living thing.

Around the House: Pick other things around the house and see if they have all five characteristics of living things.

NAME_____

Animal Charts

Use the information in the charts to answer the questions below.

Green Frog	African Elephant	Garden Spider

Type: Amphibian
Habitat: Ponds
Food: Insects
Respiration: Gills when young, develops lungs later. Gets oxygen through skin.
Reproduction: Lays thousands of eggs in water; only a few develop.
Life Cycle: Mother ignores young; young undergo metamorphosis: Egg, tadpole, adult; 2 year life span.

Type: Mammal
Habitat: Grasslands
Food: Eats 100,000 lbs. of hay and fruit a year.
Respiration: Lungs
Reproduction: Pregnancy lasts 2 years; mother has one offspring at a time.
Life Cycle: Mother cares for young, which reach maturity after 14 years; 75 year life span.

Type: Arthropod
Habitat: Land
Food: Insects
Respiration: Body tubes and book lungs.
Reproduction: Mother lays eggs in sac; eggs hatch as spiderlings.
Life Cycle: Mother takes care of spiderlings; spiderlings go through many stages called molts; 1–20 year life span.

1. Write the names of the animals on your cards that:

   a. Eat insects _____

   b. Eat plant material _____

2. Name the different ways the animals breathe. _____

_____

3. **a.** Which animals take care of their young?_____

   b. Which animals let their young survive on their own? _____

4. Which animals have life spans that are close to human life span?_____

_____

NAME _____

Anonymous Animals!

Welcome to Anonymous Animals, the game where vertebrates and invertebrates use their body forms to compete for big prizes. I'm Bob Backbone, your host. You'll use the clues to identify our Mystery Guest.

A *vertebrate* is an animal with a backbone. You are a vertebrate. An *invertebrate* has no backbone. A worm is an invertebrate.

Mystery Guest (MG): Hi Bob. Here's my first clue: I live in the sea.

MG: I have bilateral symmetry, Bob. That means that one-half of my body is a mirror image of the other half.

MG: I'm an invertebrate, Bob.

MG: I can't move from one place to another on my own. I'm motionless, Bob.

List all Animal Panel Members that:

1. live in the sea _____

   _____

2. have bilateral symmetry _____

   _____

3. are invertebrates_____

   _____

4. are motionless_____

   _____

5. Name the Mystery Guest!

   _____

Animal Panel Members

butterfly   jellyfish

sea anemone   starfish

lobster   lizard

fish   sea gull

clam   frog

Around the House: Play Animal Mystery Challenge at home! First, write four or more animal clues on index cards. Then give them to your partners and have them figure out the name of the Mystery Guest. Put each card in the pile where it belongs— vertebrate or invertebrate.

Animal "Go Fish"

Play the card game "Go Fish" using animal cards that you
make yourself. With up to three of your friends, make 32
cards, as described below. Use a reference book if you need
help. Then follow the directions to play the game.

Make these cards:
- 4 Mammals
- 4 Birds
- 4 Reptiles
- 4 Amphibians
- 4 Fish
- 4 Arthropods
- 4 Mollusks
- 4 Worms or other Invertebrates

On each card:
- Write an animal's name and draw a picture of it.
- Write whether the animal is (a) vertebrate or invertebrate,
  (b) cold-blooded or warm-blooded, (c) lives on land, water, or air,
  (d) has an exoskeleton, endoskeleton, or no skeleton.

Having trouble
remembering what all
these terms mean?
Look up each of the
following terms in the
dictionary before you
begin to play.
- vertebrates
- invertebrates
- warm-blooded
- cold-blooded
- endoskeleton
- exoskeleton

Directions:
The goal of the game is to make as many "books" as possible. A book is made
up of all four cards in any one animal category.
1. Shuffle the cards. Deal 4 cards to each player. The remaining cards are placed
   face down in a pile.
2. Each player takes turns asking the player on the left, "Do you have any
   (*mammals, birds, or another animal category*)?"
3. If the player on the left says "yes," the player asking for the card must say
   whether the animal (a) is vertebrate or invertebrate, (b) is cold-blooded or
   warm-blooded, (c) lives on land, water, or air, (d) has an exoskeleton,
   endoskeleton, or no skeleton. If the player describes the animal correctly,
   he or she gets the card.
4. If the player on the left does not have the requested card, he or she says "go
   fish." Then the first player takes a card from the pile.
5. When players make books, they put the cards in a book face up in front of
   them.
6. Play continues until one player has used all his or her cards to make books,
   with no cards left over. That player wins the game.

NAME _____

Flowering Power!

**Do plants grow best with lots of light? Take a look at the
data for this. Some of the plants flowered; some didn't.
Use the data below to answer the questions and solve
the mystery.**

It's time to
cut out the
puzzle piece
and glue or
tape it in
place on
page 64.

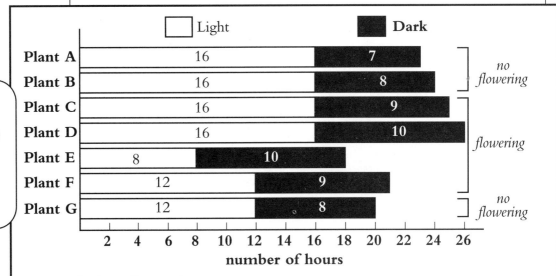

1. Which plants flowered? _____

   How many hours of light did each one receive? _____

2. Did the amount of light alone seem to determine whether a plant flowered?

   Explain your answer. _____

   _____

3. What do you notice about plants that had 9 or more hours of darkness?

   _____

4. To solve the mystery, make up a hypothesis about what plants need to flower
   based on your answer to Question 3. _____

   _____

5. Think of an experiment that would test your hypothesis. Describe the results
   you would expect. _____

   _____

   _____

12

NAME_____

Walter's Goofs

Walter is not very good with names. He has all the correct definitions for this diagram, but the names for the animal cell's parts are completely ridiculous! Fix Walter's work by picking a correct name from the box and writing it next to the wrong name for each cell part.

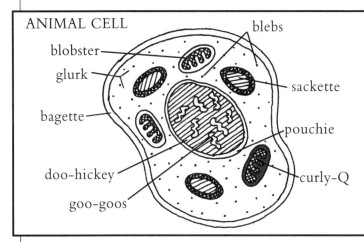

ANIMAL CELL
blebs
blobster
glurk
sackette
bagette
pouchie
doo-hickey
curly-Q
goo-goos

canal network   nuclear membrane
mitochondrion   chromosomes
cytoplasm   nucleus
vacuole   cell membrane
ribosomes

Use a dictionary or your science book if you need help.

This **blobster**_____ produces energy for the cell.

Gel called **glurk** _____ fills the inside of the cell.

Animal cells have this flexible outer covering called a **bagette** _____ .

This **doo-hickey** _____ is in the center of the cell and contains goo-goos.

The **goo-goos** _____ contain the cell's genetic information.

The **pouchie** _____ holds the doo-hickey of the cell.

These **blebs** _____ produce protein for the cell.

A **sackette** _____ stores materials for the cell.

This **curly-Q** _____ packages and moves chemicals in the cell.

NAME _____

Hit the Heights Target

To change a percent into a decimal, move the decimal point over two places to the left.
95.5 % = .955
If you have a decimal in the divisor, move the decimal point to the right as many places as it takes to make it a whole number. Be sure to move the decimal point in the dividend the same number of places.

Jenny is a 12-year-old gymnast who is 5 feet 2 inches tall. Simon is an 11-year-old basketball player who is 5 feet 0 inches tall. Jenny hopes that she won't be taller than 5 feet 7 inches as an adult. Simon hopes he won't be shorter than 6 feet 1 inch as an adult. Will they reach their goals? Look at the chart and read the explanation of how it works. Use the chart below to help you answer the questions.

Percent of Adult Height (Average)		
Age	**Boys**	**Girls**
10	78%	84.4%
11	81.1%	84.4%
12	84.2%	92.9%
13	87.3%	96.5%
14	91.5%	98.3%
15	96.1%	99.1%
16	98.3%	99.6%
17	99.3%	100%
18	99.8%	100%
19	100%	100%

How this chart works: Suppose a 10-year-old girl is 4 feet 9 inches tall; that's 57 inches. According to the chart, at age 10, this girl has reached 84.4% of her full adult height. So how do you figure what her adult height is likely to be?

number of inches tall now ÷ percent = adult height
57 inches ÷ .844 = 67.53 inches

To get her height in feet and inches:
67.53 ÷ 12 = about 5 feet $7\frac{1}{2}$ inches

1. What is Jenny's adult height likely to be?_____
   Will she reach her goal? _____

2. What is Simon's adult height likely to be? _____

3. What if Simon grows 4 inches by next year? How will this change his
   possible adult height?_____

4. According to the chart, how tall are you likely to be? _____

5. Suppose you grow 3 inches by next year. How will this change your adult-
   height prediction? _____

NAME_____

Learn About Learning

Some of our behaviors are inborn. That means we're born
with them. Other behaviors are learned. Read each
behavior below. Put a check next to your prediction. Then
follow the directions to test your predictions. Finally, write
your conclusions at the bottom of the page.

Behavior: Writing your name with your eyes closed.

Your prediction: This behavior is ——— inborn ——— learned.

1. Fold a sheet of paper down the middle.
2. With your eyes open, write your name on the left side of the paper.
3. Now close your eyes. Write your name on the right side.
4. Repeat several times. Did your eyes-closed writing seem to improve?
   _____

5. Do you think you could learn to write well with your eyes closed? Explain.
   _____
   _____

> If you laugh
> when you are
> tickled, that is
> an *inborn*
> behavior; it's
> automatic.
> Laughing at a
> joke is a
> *learned*
> behavior; you
> can decide
> whether or not
> you want
> to do it.

Behavior: Not blinking when someone claps hands in your face.

Your prediction: This behavior is ——— inborn ——— learned.

1. Have a partner clap hands 6 inches in front of your face. Try not to blink.
2. Repeat several times. Did your ability to resist blinking seem to increase?
   Explain. _____
   _____

3. Do you think you could learn to avoid blinking completely when someone
   claps? Explain. _____
   _____

Conclusion: Of the two behaviors you investigated, which do you think is
inborn? Which is learned? Explain. _____
_____
_____

NAME _____

Completely Useless?

Conduction is a measure of how well heat travels through a material. *Metals* are the best heat conductors because they let heat pass right through. *Glass* is a mid-level heat conductor. *Wood* is a poor conductor. An *insulator* like styrofoam hardly lets heat through at all.

Cut out the puzzle piece and find its place on page 64.

The Completely Useless Corporation created four new materials. The CUC scientists tested the heat conductance of the new materials and compared them to common materials. This is what they found:

Zogite = Copper   Enkon = Glass
Gryb = Wood   Porchgar = Styrofoam

The CUC scientists tried out their new materials in the products below. Rate each use of the material by checking the correct box. Then write a sentence that explains your answer.

1. A refrigerator that has zogite walls.
   ❑ very useful ❑ somewhat useful ❑ not very useful ❑ completely useless
   _____

2. A refrigerator that has porchgar walls.
   ❑ very useful ❑ somewhat useful ❑ not very useful ❑ completely useless
   _____

3. A waffle iron made of zogite.
   ❑ very useful ❑ somewhat useful ❑ not very useful ❑ completely useless
   _____

4. A waffle iron made of gryb.
   ❑ very useful ❑ somewhat useful ❑ not very useful ❑ completely useless
   _____

5. Winter boots with zogite soles and gryb uppers.
   ❑ very useful ❑ somewhat useful ❑ not very useful ❑ completely useless
   _____

6. Winter boots with porchgar soles and enkon uppers.
   ❑ very useful ❑ somewhat useful ❑ not very useful ❑ completely useless
   _____

NAME_____

Mouth Lightning

Read the "News Flash." Then try the activity below.

Dateline: Olympic Village, July 26: Hide-and-Seek superstar Ingrid Ulafson won her third straight Gold Medal today in the Free-style Hide-and-Seek competition. Ingrid's secret? "The competition was held in complete darkness this year," Ingrid says. "I gave all the other competitors wintergreen candies. Then I just looked for sparks!"

What does Ingrid mean by *looked for sparks*? To find out, follow the steps below.

Step 1 Put a wintergreen hard candy in your mouth.

Step 2 Go into a bathroom that has no windows. Or cover all windows to make the room completely dark. Then turn out the lights.

Step 3 Stand in front of a mirror and bite the candy. Keep your mouth open while you bite. Look at your mouth in the mirror. What do you see?

Now analyze your results by answering the questions.

1. When sugar crystals are broken down under extreme pressure, positive and negative charges separate. What pressure did you apply to the sugar crystals in the wintergreen candy?_____

2. When separated, positive and negative charges can jump a gap to get back together again, showing a visible electric spark. What evidence did you see of positive and negative charges jumping a gap?_____

   _____

3. The mechanical energy (biting) you applied to the candy was changed to which different form of energy?_____

4. Wintergreen candy has the property of *fluorescing,* or lighting up in the dark more than most other substances. How did biting on wintergreen candies help Ingrid in her quest for a gold medal?_____

   _____

> *Electricity* is made of tiny *positive* and *negative* charges. When the charges are separated, they try to get back together. This is what causes electricity to flow.

NAME _____

Friction or Fiction?

Read the following conversation between Chaz and his coach. Then do the experiment. Use another sheet of paper to answer the questions.

"Friction is what slows us down," Hockey star Chaz Snorter said to his coach Roger Peckman. "If it weren't for friction, we would win all our games!"

"True," said Coach Peckman. "But friction slows down both teams, Chaz, not just us."

"Hmm," Chaz said. "You may have a point there, Coach."

> Things in *motion* will stay in motion forever unless some force acts to slow them down. On Earth, *friction* and gravity are two forces that slow down almost all moving objects. Friction is the force that occurs when two objects rub against one another.

Materials:
plastic soda bottle with a top
ruler
marker
paper
scissors
ball-point pen
balloon

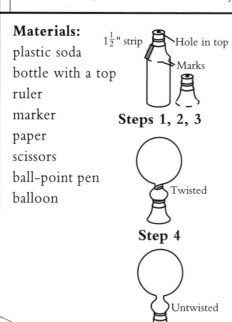

Steps 1, 2, 3

Step 4

Step 5

What To Do:

Step 1 Make marks all the way around the bottle exactly $1\frac{1}{2}$ inches below the top.

Step 2 Cut along the marks with a scissors. Make sure that the bottom edge you cut is smooth, or the experiment won't work.

Step 3 Use a ball-point pen to poke an $\frac{1}{8}$ inch hole in the top of the bottle. Push the bottle gently along a table to see how difficult it is to move.

Step 4 Blow up the balloon. Twist the balloon's neck around to keep the air inside.

Step 5 Fit the balloon's neck over the end of the bottle. When secure, untwist the balloon. Gently push the bottle along the table.

Conclusion:
1. Was the bottle easier to move before or after the filled balloon was attached? Explain.
2. The balloon shoots air down at the table. The bottle now travels on a cushion of air rather than on the table. Does this reduce or increase friction on the bottle?
3. Why is it easier to slide on ice than it is to slide on a rough floor?

NAME _____

Fossil Hunt

Professor Leaker has found fossil evidence for chimpanzees, early humans, and modern humans all living in the same site. But Prof. Leaker made a "bone-headed" mistake and put all the fossil bones in one bag. Help Prof. Leaker separate the bones. Read the description of each sample, and compare it to the fossil diagrams. Then write the name of the bag each sample belongs in. One is done for you.

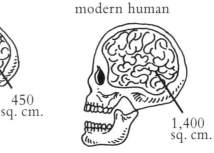

chimpanzee   early human   modern human

400 sq. cm.   450 sq. cm.   1,400 sq. cm.

Modern humans, early humans, and chimpanzees all share many traits. When scientists find their bones, they look for the traits in these diagrams.

Sample 1: This jaw has huge canine teeth. _____*chimpanzee*_____

Sample 2: The skull has a jutting eyebrow bone and a brain size of 450 sq cm. _____

Sample 3: The skull has a jutting eyebrow bone and a brain size of 400 sq cm. _____

Sample 4: This jaw has small canine teeth and a chin that sticks out.

_____

Sample 5: This jaw has small canine teeth and a chin that does not stick out. _____

Sample 6: The skull face slopes forward and the individual had large canine teeth._____

Sample 7: The skull face does not slope forward. _____

NAME _____

Paleontologist Picnic

Five paleontologists—A, B, C, D, and E—were at a picnic, bragging about their latest findings. Read about what each paleontologist found, and look at the time line that shows the different periods of Earth's history. Then answer the questions below.

The diagram shows geological time periods from the beginning of the Cambrian period to the current time.

"I found a fabulous shark fossil," said A. "It comes from the beginning of the Carboniferous period."

"Big deal," said B. "My jellyfish are 160 million years older than your shark."

"Who cares about jellyfish?" asked C. "Look at this dinosaur bone. It was buried 160 million years ago."

"Dinosaurs, dinosaurs, dinosaurs," said D. "I'm sick of dinosaurs. Check out this amphibian fossil. It's 120 million years older than C's dinosaur bone."

"My trilobite fossils are the coolest fossils of all," said E. "And they're also 100 million years older than A's shark."

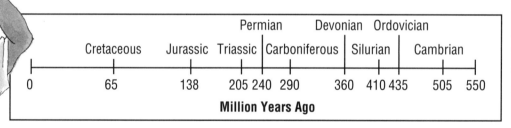

1. List the fossils in order from youngest to oldest on the lines below. Then, next to each fossil in your list, write the name of the period each fossil is from.
   a. _____ _____   d. _____ _____
   b. _____ _____   e. _____ _____
   e. _____ _____
2. Which paleontologist found a fossil from the Permian era? _____
3. Which paleontologist found a fossil from the Cambrian era?_____
4. In which period was the trilobite from? _____
5. Land plants appeared about 60 million years after the trilobite was common. How long ago did land plants first appear?_____

Here's another puzzle piece. Put it in place on page 64.

NAME_____

I Dig Dirt

We at the DURT (Dig Up Real Terrain) Society want to change people's attitudes about soil and dirt. You can help by doing each activity below using the dirt in your yard or neighborhood. Then write the answers to the questions on another sheet of paper. Tell everyone the dirt about what you learned.

Part 1: Your soil region
The map shows 11 different soil types of the United States.

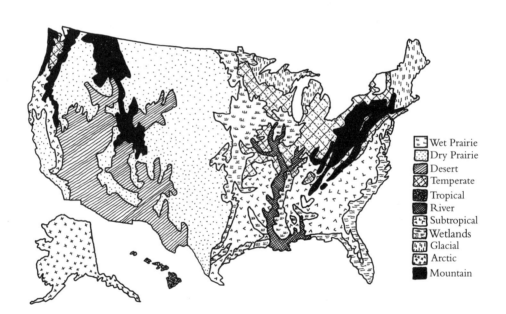

Wet Prairie
Dry Prairie
Desert
Temperate
Tropical
River
Subtropical
Wetlands
Glacial
Arctic
Mountain

ARCTIC: Thin, light in color, rocky, not very rich.

MOUNTAIN: Thin, light gray or brown, eroded.

DESERT: Coarse, sandy, does not hold water well, high in minerals.

WET/DRY PRAIRIE: Brown, dense, rich.

GLACIAL: Brown, rocky.

WETLAND: Rinsed by water but still rich and very dark.

RIVER: Very rich and dark, often contains topsoil from other lands.

TEMPERATE: Loose, brown, rich, very good for crops.

TROPICAL/SUBTROPICAL: Dark and wet.

1. What soil region do you live in? _____

NAME _____

I Dig Dirt (part two)

Soil is made of the following materials:
Gravel: large pebbles and minerals
Sand: finely ground minerals
Humus: dark material made mostly of decaying plant and animal matter
Clay: very fine mineral material that feels sticky.

Part 2: Testing your soil

A. Looking at the soil

Materials: soil, tray, magnifying glass or microscope if possible

Observe your soil. Follow the steps below.

1. Spread some soil on a tray. Describe its texture and color. Does the soil seem smooth or clumpy? Do you see gravel? sand? clay? humus? Look in the dirt for evidence of life forms, such as bugs or plants. Use a magnifying glass or microscope if you can. On another piece of paper, draw what you see.

B. Feeling the soil

Materials: soil

Feel your soil by rubbing a sample of it between your fingers.

1. If your soil feels sticky, it has a lot of clay in it. If it is gritty, it has a lot of sand in it. If it is spongy and crumbly, it has a lot of humus in it.

2. Is your soil mainly clay, sand, or humus?_____

C. Measuring the soil

Materials: soil, tall jar with a lid, water

Follow these steps to measure your soil's ingredients.

1. Fill jar $\frac{1}{4}$ full with soil. Add water so jar is $\frac{2}{3}$ full.

2. Shake hard for 2 minutes. Let settle into layers for 20 minutes or more.

3. Make some estimates: What fraction of your sample is gravel? Sand? Silt? Clay?

_____

Conclusion:

Now that you've examined your local soil, what do you think? What will you tell everyone about the characteristics of your soil? How could you find out if your soil is good for growing crops?_____

_____

_____

_____

Weather Watch

Yikes! Dan the Wacky Weather Man from TV-1 just blew up the channel's weather station! You can help by making a mini-weather station. Follow the directions to build your equipment. Keep track of the weather in the Weather Diary on page 24. Then use your weather data to answer the questions.

Measure Rain *Materials:* coffee can, ruler, masking tape	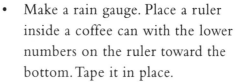	• Make a rain gauge. Place a ruler inside a coffee can with the lower numbers on the ruler toward the bottom. Tape it in place. • Check the can each day to find out how many inches of rain, snow, sleet, or hail has fallen.
Measure Wind Speed *Materials:* 3" x 5" piece of cardboard, string about 5" long, piece of sponge about 1" square, ruler, tack or push pin		• Make a wind gauge. Tie the sponge to the end of the string. Draw lines on the cardboard and mark as shown. Tack the string and the cardboard somewhere outside. • When the wind blows, look at where the string moves against the card to find wind speed.
Measure Temperature *Materials:* thermometer	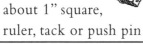	• Place a thermometer outside out of direct sunlight. • Record the temperature 2 or more times a day.
Measure Sunshine		• Look at the sky at least twice a day. • Record weather the sky is sunny or cloudy.
Keep Track of Humidity and Air Pressure		• Check the weather page of your local newspaper for these measurements.

Cut out the puzzle piece below and find where it belongs on page 64.

NAME _____

Weather Watch (part two)

Weather Diary

DAY 1　　rain: _____　temperature: _____
date:　　wind speed: _____　humidity: _____
_____　air pressure: _____　sunshine/cloudiness: _____

DAY 2　　rain: _____　temperature: _____
date:　　wind speed: _____　humidity: _____
_____　air pressure: _____　sunshine/cloudiness: _____

DAY 3　　rain: _____　temperature: _____
date:　　wind speed: _____　humidity: _____
_____　air pressure: _____　sunshine/cloudiness: _____

1. What was the highest wind speed you recorded in your Weather Diary? _____

   the lowest? _____

2. What was the greatest amount of precipitation you recorded? Was it rain, snow, or some

   other form of precipitation? _____

3. How did the temperatures you recorded compare to temperatures from the newspaper,

   radio, or TV? Did you find differences? How do you explain them? _____

   _____

4. How many times a day do you think a Weather Station should take measurements?

   At what times should they be taken? Give reasons for your anwers. _____

   _____

5. How might you use your Weather Station measurements to predict future weather?

   _____

   _____

Check Yourself: Use the radio, TV, or newspaper weather
listings to confirm the accuracy of your measurements.

NAME_____

www.energy@sun

Welcome to the World Wide Web Home
Page for the sun. It shows how the sun
supplies almost all forms of energy on
Earth. Look at each diagram. Which
form of energy is being used? Choose
from the energy box. Write the answer
on the line.

Energy Box
Electrical energy
Chemical energy
Light energy
Biological energy
Mechanical energy
Solar energy

Electrical energy comes from electric currents. *Chemical* energy often comes from burning fuels. *Light* energy comes from sources of light. *Biological* energy comes from living things. *Mechanical* energy comes from moving things. *Solar* energy comes from the sun.

Energy to Go

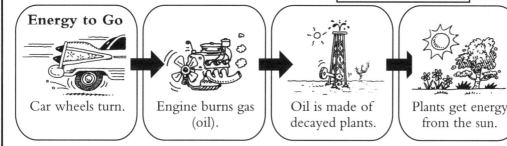

Car wheels turn. | Engine burns gas (oil). | Oil is made of decayed plants. | Plants get energy from the sun.

Mechanical Energy   Chemical Energy   _____   _____

Energy to See

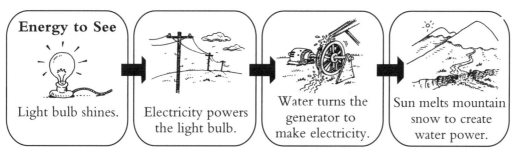

Light bulb shines. | Electricity powers the light bulb. | Water turns the generator to make electricity. | Sun melts mountain snow to create water power.

Energy to Win

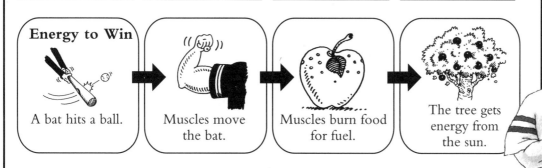

A bat hits a ball. | Muscles move the bat. | Muscles burn food for fuel. | The tree gets energy from the sun.

NAME _____

What's a Year?

In one year, the earth makes an orbit of the sun. To measure a year, you need to look to the night sky. Use the following diagram to answer the questions.

> *Constellations* are patterns of stars in the sky. The stars don't move in the sky. The zodiac is a special group of constellations that are easy to identify during different times of the year.

> Earth moves in two ways. Every day it spins in place like a top, causing day and night. It also moves in a path around the Sun over the year.

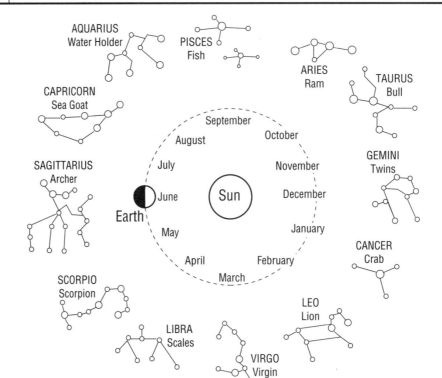

1. In June, which zodiac constellation would appear overhead? __Sagittarius__

2. In September, Earth would have completed $\frac{1}{4}$ of its trip around the sun. Which zodiac constellation would appear directly overhead?_____

3. In December, what fraction of Earth's trip around the sun would be complete? Which constellation would appear directly overhead?_____

4. In March, what fraction of Earth's trip around the sun would be complete? Which constellation would appear directly overhead?_____

5. After 12 months, which constellation would be in view? How would you know that a year had passed?_____

NAME_____

Believe It Or Not!

This page will amaze and confuse you! Read each pair of
sentences. Your job is to separate the TRUE from the
FALSE. Write TRUE or FALSE on the line before each
number.

_____ 1. Alexander Graham Bell made the world's first **telephone** call when he used his
invention to call for help after spilling battery acid on his pants.

_____ 2. Alexander Graham Bell made the world's first **telephone** call when he called for a
pizza using his new invention.

_____ 3. In the 3rd century B.C., the Greek scientist Archimedes was in the bathtub when he
discovered the principle of **floating.** He ran through the streets shouting "Eureka!" to
celebrate his discovery.

_____ 4. In the 3rd century B.C., the Greek scientist Archimedes discovered the **transistor radio**
while sitting in his bathtub. He ran through the streets shouting "Eureka!" to celebrate
his discovery.

_____ 5. The **parachute** was first designed in 1845 by Italian painter Leonardo da Crashi who
completed several famous paintings while falling through the air.

_____ 6. The **parachute** was first designed in 1485 by Italian painter Leonardo da Vinci who is
perhaps better known for painting the *Mona Lisa.*

_____ 7. To test the safety of his new invention, Elisha Otis had the support ropes of the
elevator he was riding cut. The safety system worked, and Otis was not hurt.

_____ 8. To test the safety of his new invention, Elisha Otis lived in an **elevator** for one entire
year without eating or drinking.

_____ 9. In 1780, Luigi Galvani discovered **electricity** in a dead frog's leg.

_____ 10. In 1780, Luigi Galvani discovered a **mini-computer** in a dead frog's leg.

_____ 11. The **zipper** was invented by Zippy "the Lip" Zipfield in 1981 as a device for holding
broken banana peels together.

_____ 12. The **zipper,** invented by Whitcomb Judson in 1891, was not widely used until the U.S.
Navy put it on flying suits during World War I. The device was not given the name
"zipper" until 1926.

NAME _____

Tricky Traps

Having trouble getting started? Think of what your device needs:
(1) a way to reach into the corner
(a long arm?);
(2) a trap;
(3) something to view the hamsters (a mirror? a camera?);
(4) some way to pull the hamsters back once they are caught.

It's time again to put a puzzle piece in place. You know what to do.

The hamsters in the Science Lab have escaped! They're hiding in a corner behind a really heavy box. Your job is to design a device that will:

- **Reach the corner where the hamsters are hiding.**
- **View the hamsters.**
- **Catch the hamsters without injuring them.**

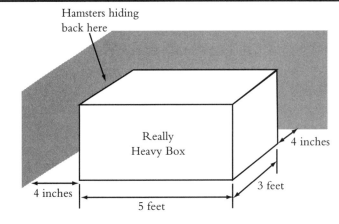

Hamsters hiding back here

Really Heavy Box

4 inches

4 inches

5 feet

3 feet

1. Give your device a name. _____

2. Describe the materials you will use to make it. _____

_____

_____

_____

3. Explain how it will work. _____

_____

_____

_____

4. Draw a plan for your device.

NAME

Jack and Jill Revisited

Attention: all police units. Bike riders answering to the names of "Jack" and "Jill" were last seen riding up a hill unarmed, unsafe, and in violation of several safety rules. The following sing-along verses were found near the scene. Read each one. Then list the safety rules that were broken. The first one has been started for you.

Jack and Jill rode up the hill
On a hot day without any (sunblock or) water.
Jack fell down (he forgot to signal a turn),
And broke his crown (of his baseball cap),
And Jill came tumbling after.

1. **Safety rules broken:**
   no bicycle helmets
   no hand signals

Jan and Jake swam in the lake
Alone, after a big lunch, in deep water.
Jan dove down (into a shallow, rocky area),
She hoped not to drown,
And Jake came plunging after.

2. **Safety rules broken:**

Jane and Bill sledded down the hill
Into a pond with half-frozen water.
Jane sledded down (without coat or hat),
Her face a frown,
And Bill came barreling after.

3. **Safety rules broken:**

Around the House: Look around your house for safety features. Do you have smoke detectors? Do they have fresh batteries? Is there a fire extinguisher in your home? What other features can you find?

NAME _____

Shrink 'n' Travel

Directions

1. Step into the Shrink 'n' Travel Machine.
2. Fasten your seatbelt.
3. Set the dial to SHRINK.
4. In 10 seconds, you will shrink down to microscopic size.
5. Go on the tour of Human Body Systems. When you get back, answer the questions.

Digestive System

Main functions:
- Breaks down food.
- Eliminates waste.

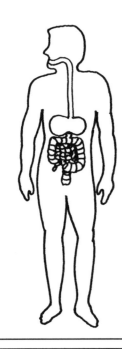

Links
- The digestive system delivers digested food to the circulatory system.
- The circulatory system delivers digested food to cells in all body systems.
- Cells burn food using oxygen from respiratory system.

Circulatory System

Main function:
- Transports food, oxygen and chemicals to body cells.

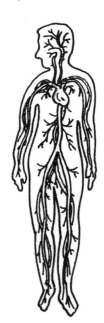

Links
- Food and oxygen to cells from the respiratory and digestive systems.
- Blood to all body systems, including nervous, skeletal/ muscular, and reproductive systems.
- Chemicals from hormone system to other body systems.

NAME

Shrink 'n' Travel (part two)

Skeletal/Muscular System

Main functions:

- Allows body movement.
- Body support.

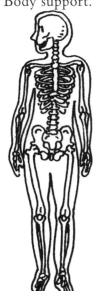

Links

- Skeleton protects other body systems.
- Muscles cause movement in digestive system.
- Heart muscle produces heartbeat in circulatory system.

Respiratory System

Main functions:

- Delivers oxygen to body systems.

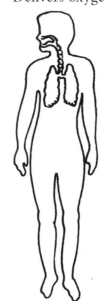

Links

- The respiratory system delivers oxygen to the circulatory system.
- The circulatory system carries oxygen to all body systems.
- Cells use oxygen to burn food from digestive system.

> A *body system* is a group of organs and tissues that perform a function for the body. There are other body systems besides the ones listed here. Each body system also has many more functions and links to other body systems than those shown.

1. Which body system seems to have the most links to other systems? Explain.

   _____

2. What three systems work together to bring food and oxygen to the body's cells so they can get energy? _____

3. What system works together with the nervous system to allow you to kick a ball?

   _____

4. Suppose your nervous system wasn't working correctly. What effects might you see in other body systems?_____

   _____

5. Which body system seems to have the fewest links to other systems? Explain.

   _____

   _____

NAME _____

Junk Food Alert

Get a package of junk food. Look at the Nutrition Facts and Ingredients List. Then, write a junk food warning of your own. Fill in the box below to make your own "Warning Label."

Calories tell you how much food energy an item has. *Fat* is a part of food that is rich in calories. Too much fat is unhealthy. Each category on the food label tells the percent of the daily recommended value that one serving will supply.

Cut out the puzzle piece. Glue or tape it in place on page 64.

NAME

The Evidence, Please

To prove a hypothesis, you have to get as much evidence as possible. Then you have to analyze the evidence to decide what is most convincing. Look at the hypothesis and evidence in the chart. Then follow the directions.

Hypothesis: Dogs are smarter than cats.	
Evidence For	**Evidence Against**
Interviews: Dog owners say dogs are smarter.	**Interviews:** Cat owners say cats are smarter.
Observation: Dogs catch Frisbees.	**Observation:** Cats catch mice.
Experiment: Dog followed command to get food.	**Experiment:** Cat ignored command and got food anyway.
Research: Dog magazine says dogs have a higher IQ.	**Research:** Cat magazine says cats are more intelligent.

Evidence is anything that proves or disproves your hypothesis. It can be in the form of experiments, observations, measurements, interviews, or research materials.

1. Put stars next to the evidence in your chart that supports the hypothesis. Put Xs next to the evidence that goes against it.

2. Which evidence do you think is more convincing? Why?

_____

Circle a hypothesis on the list below. On another sheet of paper, make a chart to show evidence for and against the hypothesis. Then answer the questions below.

Pizza is America's favorite food.   Computers help kids learn in school.
TV violence makes kids   Dogs are friendlier than cats.
more violent.

3. Which evidence supports your hypothesis?_____

4. Which evidence goes against your hypothesis? _____

5. Overall, which evidence is more convincing? Why?_____

_____

NAME _____

Space IDs

The crew of the starship *S.S. Pegasus* needs new ID cards. Your job is to give each crew member a classification: Human, Clone, Android, or Robot. Read the description of each classification. Then read the descriptions of the crew members. Write a classification for each crew member on the line.

	Human	Clone	Android	Robot
Brain Power	Level 5–9	Level 5–9	Level 4–10	Level 1–10
Emotional Range	Level 6–10	Level 6–10	Level 3–8	Level 1–4
Body Material	Flesh and blood	Flesh and blood	Flesh and blood, plastic	Metal, plastic
Body Type	One-of-a-kind	Copy	One-of-a-kind or copy	One-of-a-kind or copy

Each trait rated on a Level 1 to Level 10 scale.

Bob Barski, Gyro-Programmer: Good chess player with level-7 brain power, but emotional rating of 7 makes him hate to lose. Has 7 identical brothers. Underwent replacement of only his plastic body material 2 years ago.

*Classification:*_____

Jemma Urbb, Technical Specialist: Volleyball player injured 6 months ago. Highest brain power (level 9) makes her ideal leader. Has no brothers or sisters. Talented artist with level-9 emotional rating.

*Classification:*_____

Major-Doctor 47-P5 Howard: Doctor who specializes in heart surgery. Emotional level 6 makes him cool under pressure. He is the 47th copy of a human named Howard Huge.

Classification: _____

Mary Jean Felkins, Bio-Administrator: Specialist in cooking with brain power of level 5 and emotional rating of level 2. Beloved by crew for her tasty omelets and spectacular blueberry pie.

Classification: _____

NAME_____

Roundie or Boxer?

Suppose buglike creatures landed in your neighborhood. What would you call them? Read the rules for naming these creatures. Then follow the directions below.

Shape
- A Roundie has a round body and round eyes.
- A Boxie has a square body and square eyes.
- A Rounder has a round body and square eyes.
- A Boxer has a square body and round eyes.

Body Color and Tail Type
- The first color in the name indicates body color—blue or green.
- The second color indicates eye color—blue or green.
- Body color and eye color must never be the same.
- Curly or straight refers to tail type.

Now help your neighbors identify these creatures from their descriptions. Write the name of each creature on the line. Then draw it in the space.

1. straight tail, round green body, blue square eyes

   _____

2. curly tail, square blue body, square green eyes

   _____

3. straight tail, round blue body, round green eyes

   _____

4. curly tail, square green body, square blue eyes

   _____

NAME

Rabbits and Foxes

In nature's food chain some animals are prey and others are the predators that eat the prey. The game Rabbits and Foxes is based on this fact. Foxes are predators. Rabbits are prey. Here's how to play:

You'll Need
- 2 players
- Game board
- 2 dice
- 10 playing pieces for each player

Safe   **Safe**

1. The object of the game for foxes is to catch rabbits. For rabbits, the object of the game is to escape from foxes.

2. Decide who will be rabbits and who will be foxes. Start with 1 rabbit and 1 fox at GO. Rabbits uses 2 dice; foxes, 1 die. Rabbit always goes first.

3. Both players take turns rolling the dice. The fox catches the rabbit by landing on or passing the rabbit's square.

4. Each time a rabbit passes GO, it reproduces. That means that another rabbit playing piece is added to the board on GO. A fox reproduces every 3rd time it passes GO—but only if it has caught at least one rabbit during that time.

5. Rabbits are safe from foxes in the SAFE square. A rabbit may stay in a SAFE square for 2 turns only. If more than one rabbit is on the board, at least one rabbit must move each turn.

6. If foxes catch all rabbits, the foxes win. If a fox goes 6 times around the board without catching any rabbits, it runs out of food. Then the rabbits win.

Go →   **Safe**

NAME_____

Food Chain Super Store

At Food Chain, foods are arranged according to their place
in the food chain. That means at Food Chain you'll get a
dazzling variety of top quality Producers, tasty Primary
Consumers, scrumptious Secondary Consumers, and
delectable Decomposers. Help the Food Chain Super Store
organize its merchandise. Look at the pictures below. Pick
life forms that would make up a food chain, and draw them
in place in the space below. (You don't have to use all the
pictures.) Draw arrows to show who eats what. Then label
each picture as a *producer, primary consumer, secondary consumer,*
or a *decomposer.*

Definition Box

A *food chain* shows
who eats what.
A *producer* is a plant
that makes food.
A *primary consumer* is
an animal that eats
only producers.
A *secondary consumer*
is an animal that eats
other consumers.
A *decomposer* is a life
form that breaks down
dead matter.

Here's the puzzle
piece. Put it in
place on page 64. Is
the puzzle taking
shape yet?

NAME _____

Johnny Heartthrob

Mutualism: when both parties are helped by a relationship. *Commensalism:* when one party is helped by a relationship, and the other party is not affected. *Parasitism:* when one party is helped by a relationship, and the other party is harmed. *Predation:* when one party eats the other party.

The world of Johnny Heartthrob—mega rock star— is complicated. It's filled with the same kind of relationships found in a biological community. Read about the relationship each person below has with Johnny Heartthrob. Write *mutualism, commensalism, parasitism,* or *predation* to identify the kind of relationship.

Johnny Heartthrob: He's the mega rock star, with multi-platinum CDs, Grammies, Oscars, million-dollar shoe endorsements, and even his own fragrance—O' Da Johnny!

Nancy Heartthrob: Johnny's sister. She has used the Heartthrob name to land a key part in a hit TV series. Johnny's own CD sales don't seem to be affected by Nancy's success.

_____

Sid Porshay: Johnny's agent. The best agent in show biz. Sid always gets Johnny the best deal. She is also one of the wealthiest agents in show biz, as she gets a healthy cut of every deal that she makes for Johnny.

_____

Larry Foznik: Johnny's ex-manager. Why did Johnny ever hire this guy? All he ever did was set up lousy deals for Johnny. Larry got all the money. Johnny got all the trouble.

_____

Jack Rabbit Records: Johnny's record company. It started out as a tiny company. Since then it has bought out and taken over several other major music companies. Now it's one of the biggest music companies in show biz.

_____

Toni Thresh: Runs the Johnny Heartthrob Impersonator School. Toni teaches Johnny wannabes to be "just like Johnny." It's made her a fortune, and many of her students have gone on to be successful Johnny impersonators. Impersonators seem to increase Johnny's popularity.

_____

Jonnie Throbhart: Johnny's most successful impersonator. Jonnie has become a major Las Vegas act himself, putting a humorous spin on the character of the real Johnny. What does the real Johnny think of Jonnie's act? "It doesn't bother me!" he says.

_____

NAME_____

Nature vs. Environment

Where did you get your ability to play sports? Did you learn it from practicing a lot? Did you inherit it from your parents, who are both terrific athletes? Or is it a little of both? Read each trait in the box. Write it in where you think it goes on the Nature/Environment line. One is done for you.

Something that you learned is said to be controlled by environment. Something that you inherited is controlled by nature. In most cases, there is no single right answer to questions of nature versus environment.

eye color
musical ability
running speed
intelligence
fear of snakes
eye color
nose shape
hair type
favorite ice cream
interest in science
taste in clothes
interest in sports
neatness
personality
height
shoe size
sense of humor
honesty
body strength

Nature

eye color —|—

Environment

Around the House: Have family members put the traits on their own nature/environment lines. Does everyone agree?

NAME

Biome Top 3 Lists

Look at the map below. It shows the earth's major biomes. Use the map to find the location of each biome on your Top 3 lists on the next page. Then write the names of animals and plants that live in the different biomes. Look in an encyclopedia or reference book if you need help. Some examples are given for you. After you finish these, you can make your own Top 3 lists for the other biomes on the map.

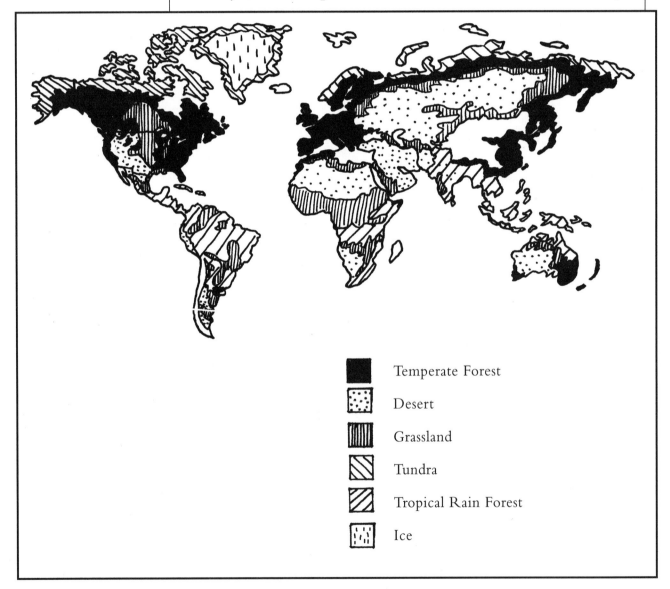

■ Temperate Forest

▦ Desert

▥ Grassland

▧ Tundra

▨ Tropical Rain Forest

▦ Ice

40

NAME_____

Largest Deserts

1. Africa

2. Australia

3. _____

Desert Animals

1. lizards

2. _____

3. _____

Desert Plants

1. cactus

2. _____

3. _____

Largest Rain Forests

1. _____

2. _____

3. _____

Rain Forest Animals

1. butterflies

2. _____

3. _____

Rain Forest Plants

1. vines

2. _____

3. _____

Largest Grasslands

1. _____

2. _____

3. _____

Grasslands Animals

1. _____

2. _____

3. _____

Grasslands Plants

1. _____

2. _____

3. _____

A *biome* is a very large area in which similar ecosystems and climates exist. To help identify each biome, you might write the name of a country that is located in that biome.

Your Top 3 lists were really tops! Now for some top-notch fun, cut out your puzzle piece and paste it on page 64.

NAME _____

Phantom Flies

Read about the imaginary Phantom Fly. Then read each situation. Use the information about Phantom Flies to complete the diagrams and answer the questions.

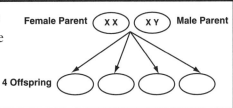

- Phantom Flies reproduce both sexually and asexually.
- Phantom Fly females each have two X chromosomes.
- Phantom Fly males each have one X and one Y chromosome.
- Phantom Flies always have four offspring when they reproduce.

Sexual reproduction: cells from two parents fuse to become a baby. *Asexual reproduction:* a parent cell makes a copy of itself. *Chromosomes:* genetic material inside cells that decides traits. X and Y chromosomes determine sex. A girl has two X chromosomes in each cell. A boy has one X and one Y chromosome in each cell.

Situation 1: A female reproduces *asexually.* This diagram shows the gender of the offspring that result.

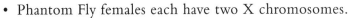

Female Parent (X X)

4 Offspring (X X) (X X) (X X) (X X)

Situation 2: A male and a female reproduce *sexually.* Each offspring gets one chromosome from its mother and one chromosome from its father. Draw all four possibilities of offspring.

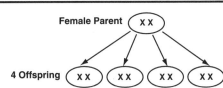

Female Parent (X X) (X Y) Male Parent

4 Offspring ◯ ◯ ◯ ◯

Situation 3: A male reproduces *asexually.* What genders of offspring will result? Draw all four possibilities.

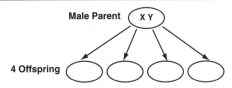

Male Parent (X Y)

4 Offspring ◯ ◯ ◯ ◯

1. Look at Situation 1. How many male offspring resulted from asexual reproduction? How many female offspring?_____

2. In Situation 2, how many males and females resulted from sexual reproduction?_____

3. In Situation 3, how many female and male offspring resulted from asexual reproduction?_____

4. What do you conclude about sexual and asexual reproduction? Which gives a greater variety of offspring?_____

42

NAME_____

Freezer Filler

Hedda and Fredda ordered a dozen Ultimate Gourmet Ice Cubes. When the cubes arrived, they had melted, and each cube-case was only partly filled. Hedda and Fredda know that ice turns into water when its temperature goes above 32°F. But the cube cases were only partially filled with water. Should Hedda and Fredda send the cubes back? Make up an experiment to find out. Gather the materials listed below. Then write a hypothesis and complete the experiment outline. Answer the questions on another piece of paper.

Ultimate Cubes Gourmet Ice Cubes

The very best in the world.
Imported from France
Only $9.95 a dozen

Each ice cube is individually packed in its own genuine plastic cube-case for your protection.

Having trouble beginning your experiment?
• Put some water in a small plastic container. Mark its height on the container and then freeze the water. See if the height changes.
• Here's another idea. Mark the height of frozen water in a container. Let it melt, and then mark the new height. Did the level change?

Materials:
Water
Plastic containers
Freezer

Hypothesis:
Write a hypothesis._____
_____

Experimental Plan:
Write a step-by-step plan to test your hypothesis. _____
_____
_____
_____
_____

Results:
Write the results of your experiment here. _____
_____
_____
_____
_____

Analysis:
1. Does water change size when it freezes? If so, in what way?
2. Do you think that water also changes size when it melts? If so, in what way?
3. How could you test your answer to question 1?
4. Should Hedda and Fredda send back their ice cubes? Or will refreezing solve their problem? Explain.

NAME _____

Oh, Goody!

You can answer question 1 by finding the difference of the bag in weight before and after Arky used the magnet to pull out the iron chips. If you add the weight of all the parts of the Goody Bag, you should get the total weight of the Goody Bag.

Good Job! Cut out the puzzle piece and put it in place on page 64.

Arkansas Smith, the famous archaeologist, discovered a Goody Bag from an ancient birthday party that took place over 3,000 years ago. He analyzed the bag and all of the stuff in it. Use the information from his analysis to answer the questions.

Step 1   Arky poured water into the contents of the bag to dissolve all the sugar inside. After the water and sugar were gone the bag weighed 180 grams.

Step 2   Arky held a magnet to the bag and pulled out all the iron chips. The bag now weighed 128 grams.

Step 3   Arky poured the contents of the bag through a large-holed filter. Only very large lead chips stayed in the filter. The rest of the materials poured through. The bag now weighed 64 grams.

Step 4   Arky filtered the bag again through a smaller-holed filter. This time he collected sand in the filter. Left in the bag were 16 grams of pure gold dust! "Eureka!" Arky cried.

1. What was the weight of the iron chips in the bag? _____

2. What was the weight of the lead chips in the bag? _____

3. What was the weight of the sand in the bag? _____

4. What was the weight of the gold dust in the bag? _____

5. Arky found that the sugar in Step 1 weighed 36 grams. How much did the entire Goody Bag weigh? _____

NAME_____

Holes in the Water

Suppose you had a glass of water that was full to the brim.
Then you added 2 spoonfuls of new material to the glass.
The glass would overflow, right? In fact, no matter what
you added to that full glass, it would cause the water to
overflow. Or would it? Try these experiments to find out.
Write your results on the lines. Answer the conclusion
questions on another piece of paper.

Materials:

paper or plastic cup   water   teaspoon

paper towels   pebbles or gravel   sugar

Experiment 1: Put the cup on some paper towels. Then pour water to the
very top of the cup. Very carefully add 1 spoonful of pebbles. After the water
settles, add a second spoonful of pebbles.

Write the results: _____

_____

Experiment 2: Put the cup on some paper towels. Pour water to the very
top of the cup. Very carefully add 1 spoonful of sugar. Wait for the sugar to
dissolve. After the water settles, add a second spoonful of sugar and wait for it
to dissolve.

Write the results: _____

_____

> Be sure to add the pebbles and sugar to the water slowly and carefully. Give the sugar time to dissolve before you add more.

> When a substance dissolves in a liquid, it can change the properties of the liquid.

Conclusions:

1. Describe the difference between adding pebbles and adding sugar to the
    water.
2. When something dissolves in water, the solution turns clear. Which of
    the two substances dissolved in water?
3. When a substance dissolves in water, it finds "holes" between molecules
    where it fits in. Use this "hole" idea to explain what happened in these
    experiments. Which substance found "holes?" What evidence do you have
    that it fit between these holes?
4. What do you think dissolving has to do with finding "holes" in water?
    Explain.

NAME _____

Energy Balloon

One important form of energy is heat energy. When
something is heated, its molecules move faster. Can speedy
molecules make a paper spiral move? Try this activity with
an adult to find out. Then answer the questions.

There are many
forms of energy,
including
heat energy,
electrical energy,
chemical energy,
light energy,
nuclear energy,
sound energy,
and
mechanical energy.

Nice job!
Here's another
puzzle piece. You
know what to do.

Step 1   Trace the shape below onto another piece of paper. Cut it out on
the dashed lines to make a paper spiral.

Step 2   Poke a small hole at the X. Put a thread through the hole, and tie it.

Step 3   Hold the spiral by the string above a heat source such as a hot
radiator or heated hot plate. What happens?

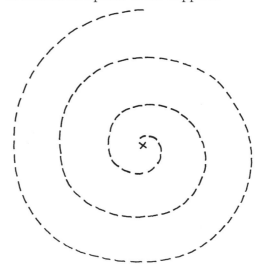

Analyze Your Results:

1. Heat makes molecules move faster. What happened to the air molecules
above the heat source?_____

_____

How could you tell? _____

2. If you were in a hot air balloon, what would you do to make the balloon
go higher? lower?_____

_____

3. In this activity, heat energy changed into what form of energy?_____

_____

46

NAME_____

Crooked Light

Edith Edge, a worker at the Bureau of Utterly Weird Happenings, got a call from a guy who saw some crooked light. Now, Edith knows light travels in straight lines. But the guy told Edith to try the experiment below. He said it would demonstrate a form of crooked light called *refraction*. Follow the directions to perform the experiment. Then answer the questions below.

When light moves through one substance, like air, to another, like liquid, it changes speed. This change in speed causes light to bend. The bending of light is called *refraction*.

Materials:
flashlight, two 3" x 5" pieces of heavy paper or cardboard, scissors, square-sided bottle such as a juice or olive bottle with a lid, drops of milk

Step 1 Cut a slit about $\frac{1}{8}$ of an inch wide in each card.

Step 2 Fill the bottle with water. Add a few drops of milk to better see the light bend. Screw the lid on the bottle.

Step 3 Hold the bottle at an angle. Darken the room, and shine the light through the slits and the bottle.

Path of Light

Conclusion:

1. Was the claim of "crooked" light correct? Why or why not?_____

_____

2. Take away the bottle and try shining the light through the slits. Do you still see refraction? Explain. _____

_____

3. Describe refraction in your own words. _____

4. What makes refraction occur?_____

_____

5. Name some other situations in which you might see refraction. _____

_____

NAME _____

A Light Tantrum

The World's Greatest Actor, Count Leo Von Herkimer, is hopping mad. "I ordered **WHITE** light for my big close-up scene," the Count says to his director, Diane Lux. "Not **COLORED** light."

"But Count," Diane says. "White light is a *mixture* of colored light, and I can prove it."

Help Diane prove it by doing the following experiment. Then answer the questions.

A *prism* breaks white light into a rainbow of colors.

Maybe the disk turned more of a gray color than white. But if you could color the colors in just the right shades, you would get a perfect white color when you spun the disk.

Here's the next puzzle piece. Put it in place on page 64.

Materials:

round white piece of cardboard or heavy paper; red, orange, yellow, green, blue, and purple crayons; pencil

Step 1   Divide the disk into 6 equal sections.

Step 2   Color each section a different color: red, orange, yellow, purple, green, and blue.

Step 3   Poke a hole in the center of the circle. Push a pencil into the hole and spin it like a top.

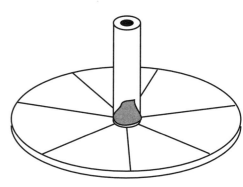

Conclusion:

1. What color did the disk turn when you spun it rapidly?_____

2. Who was right—Diane or the Count?_____

3. What colors is white made of?_____

4. Suppose you combined all colors of light except red and green. Do you think they would combine to form white? Explain your answer.

_____

_____

_____

_____

NAME_____

Pool Science

"Pool is all science," says famous pool player Minnesota Slim. "Force and motion tell you where the ball will go." Slim has a couple of experiments that prove his point. Do each one. Then use the results to answer the questions on the next page.

Materials:

3 tennis balls (or other balls of same size) numbered so you can tell them apart

Use the numbered balls to perform the three experiments. Begin each experiment by placing Ball 1 on the same spot on a table.

Experiment 1: Force from One Direction

1. Knock Ball 2 into Ball 1 from the left. Then knock Ball 1 from the right.

2. In each case, in which direction does Ball 1 move? _____

   _____

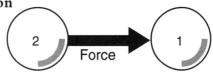

Experiment 2: Force from Two Opposite Directions

1. Use Ball 2 and Ball 3 to apply equal forces at the *same time* on Ball 1 from two opposite directions—left and right—as shown.

2. In which direction does Ball 1 move?

   _____

   _____

NAME _____

Pool Science (part two)

1. How did you apply forces to Ball 1? _____

2. If you apply a force to a ball from the right, in what direction will the ball travel? _____

   If you apply a force from the left? _____

   From below? _____

   From above? _____

3. Make up a rule that summarizes the information in question 2. _____

   _____

   _____

4. If you apply two equal forces to a ball in opposite directions at the very same time, in what direction will the ball travel? Explain. _____

   _____

5. If you apply two equal forces to a ball from below and right, what do you think will happen to the ball? _____

   _____

6. How do two separate forces combine to create one force on an object? Explain. _____

   _____

   _____

7. Was Minnesota Slim correct? Do pool balls really behave according to the forces applied to them? Explain. _____

   _____

   _____

A *force* is an
action that
changes the
speed and the
direction of an
object.

Around the House: What other sports involve forces acting on objects? How many can you name? For each sport, make a list that identifies the force and the object it acts on. Discuss your list with the sports fans in your family.

NAME_____

Problems with #7

Victor Chabrol designs what he calls the world's finest umbrellas. Victor is having trouble attaching his latest model Blob #7's top to its handle. He needs to attach the handle at the umbrella's *balance point,* or center of gravity. But how does he find it? Help Victor by doing the experiment below. Then answer the questions.

Materials:

cardboard or heavy paper; ball-point pen; bulletin board or another surface to tack things; tack, push pin, or straight pin; string with a paper clip tied to one end

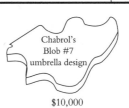

Chabrol's Blob #7 umbrella design

$10,000

Step 1 Draw Blob #7 on the cardboard. Cut it out.

Step 2 Use a pen to poke 4 or more holes anywhere along the edge of Blob #7.

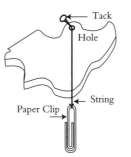

Tack

Hole

String

Paper Clip

Step 3 Put the tack through one of the holes, and tack Blob #7 to the bulletin board. Tie the free end of the string to the tack. Let the paper clip fall and the string hang freely. Trace a line along the edge of the string.

Step 4 Repeat step 3 with each hole in Blob #7. Then make an X where the lines intersect. This is the center of gravity.

Gravity pulls on the entire umbrella, as if all of its weight were focused on one point. This point is called the *center of gravity.* Objects will balance on their center of gravity.

Don't forget to cut out the puzzle piece and put it where it belongs.

1. Test the center of gravity. Put the top of your finger in the center of Blob #7 and try to balance it. Does it balance? _____

2. Try balancing Blob #7 at other parts on its surface. Does it balance?_____

    What do you conclude about the center of gravity?_____

3. Make your own shape out of cardboard. Find its center of gravity. Test the center of gravity by balancing it on your finger. Describe your results.

    _____

    _____

NAME _____

Phases of the Moon

Why is the Moon sometimes a crescent, then a half circle, then a whole circle? And what does all this have to do with tides here on Earth? Read the paragraphs about the moon and tides. Then perform the demonstration to make a model of the Moon's phases and tides.

Gravity on the Moon and Sun pull on Earth. They cause water in the oceans to "bulge." The bulge appears twice a day as *tides.* The tides are strongest when both the Sun and Moon are lined up, and the gravity of both the Sun and Moon pull on Earth.

Materials:

white styrofoam ball with pencil stuck in it, 100 watt (or brighter) lamp

Step 1 You are Earth. Place the lamp (Sun) in the center of a dark room. Hold the ball (Moon) directly in front of you. No part of the "Moon" should appear bright.

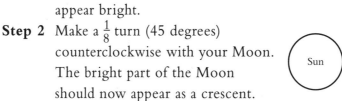

Step 2 Make a $\frac{1}{8}$ turn (45 degrees) counterclockwise with your Moon. The bright part of the Moon should now appear as a crescent.

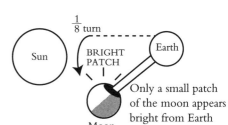

Step 3 Keep making $\frac{1}{8}$ turns all the way around Earth.

Write the answers to the questions on the lines.

1. At which positions did the Moon appear as a crescent?_____

_____

2. At which position did you see a half Moon?_____

_____

3. At which position did you see a full Moon? When did you see no Moon at all? _____

_____

4. At what moon phase would you expect the highest tides on Earth? Explain your answer. _____

_____

NAME_____

Make a Volcano

Hi, Charles Igneous here for Igneous Rocks, the world's
most popular and durable rocks. They have all the minerals
you need and contain no fats or artificial preservatives. And
now, we at Igneous present a reenactment of how igneous
rocks are formed. We call it Make a Volcano. You can do it,
too. Just follow the directions. Then answer the questions.

Materials:
narrow-necked bottle, dirt, 1 Tbsp. liquid dish detergent, a few drops of red
food coloring, 1 cup vinegar, warm water, 2 Tbsp. baking soda

Step 1   Work outside. Build a mound of dirt around the bottle so only the
very top of the bottle neck shows.

Step 2   Put the detergent, vinegar, and food coloring in the bottle. Then add
enough warm water to almost reach the top.

Step 3   Mix the baking soda in a small amount of water. Add the mixture to
the bottle. Then stand back and watch.

Questions:

1. Real volcanos occur when there is a weakness in Earth's crust. The intense
heat from inside Earth builds up pressure. What was the source of pressure
for the volcano you made? _____

_____

_____

2. Real volcanos build up pressure when their vent, or hole, is covered. What
do you think would happen if you sealed the top of your volcano?

_____

_____

3. Compare your "magma" to real magma. How are the two different? How
are they the same?_____

_____

_____

Igneous rocks
are rocks that
come from the
inside Earth.
There, super-hot
temperatures
melt the rock,
turning it into
magma. The
magma may come
out of Earth
through a
volcano. When
magma cools,
it becomes
igneous rock.

NAME _____

Rockin' Fairy Tale

Sandstone is a *sedimentary rock*. Sedimentary rocks are laid down gradually over millions of years as layers of sand, mud, silt, and minerals. Pressure squeezes sedimentary rocks together.

Rock on! Here's another puzzle piece. You know what to do.

Read the rockin' fairy tale below. Then follow the directions to make sandstone.

Once upon a time, there was a happy quartz crystal. Millions of years passed. Wind and weather ground the quartz into sand. But it was still happy. Millions of years passed again. The sand had turned to sandstone. How did this happen? To find out, follow the directions below.

Materials:

clean empty 1 cup milk carton; sand or dirt; flour; water; something to use as a weight, such as a food can or a small brick

Step 1 Cut off the top of the milk carton. Pour a layer of sand about $\frac{1}{2}$ inch deep into the carton bottom.

Step 2 Make the cement that will hold the sandstone together. Mix $\frac{1}{4}$ cup flour into 1 cup of water until it becomes a thin paste. Add the paste to the sand in the carton. Stir and let settle.

Step 3 Cut a piece from the milk carton top to make a square that fits inside the milk carton. Place the brick or weight on the square and push down hard to pack down the sand layer. Remove the square and allow the sandstone layer to dry overnight.

Step 4 When the layer is dry, pour a new layer on top. Repeat to make as many layers of sandstone as you want. When all the layers are dry, cut the milk carton away from the sandstone.

Questions:

1. How is the sandstone you made similar to real sandstone? How is it different?

_____

_____

2. Lower layers of sedimentary rock are often harder than upper layers. Why do you think this is?_____

_____

3. Some sedimentary rocks are hard; others are relatively soft. What do you think might cause sedimentary rocks to be hard or soft?_____

_____

NAME_____

Highly Unlikely

Read the information about the game Highly Unlikely. Then follow the directions, and use the climate profile graphs to solve the problems on page 56.

Climate is a long-term weather pattern. The climate of a place tells you whether it is generally warm or cold, wet or dry.

It's time to play **Highly Unlikely**, the game of highly unlikely situations. **Which of these situations do you find most unlikely?**

A. Weird green aliens visit Los Angeles on a sunny day in July.
B. Weird green aliens visit Los Angeles on a rainy day in July.
C. Weird green aliens visit Los Angeles on a snowy day in July.

Three main things affect climate:
• The closer a place is to the equator, the warmer its climate.
• Water tends to make climates mild.
• High elevation makes for colder, drier, windier climates.

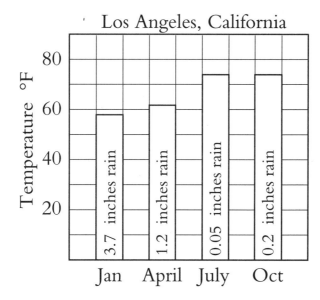

Los Angeles, California

Weird green aliens would never visit Los Angeles on a snowy day in July. Los Angeles has a warm climate. You'd almost never see a snowy day in Los Angeles in July.

NAME _____

Highly Unlikely (part two)

Use the climate profiles to decide whether each situation is **LIKELY, SOMEWHAT LIKELY, UNLIKELY,** or **HIGHLY UNLIKELY.** Write and explain your answers. The first one is done for you.

1. Minneapolis will hold a water skiing race in April.

   <u>HIGHLY UNLIKELY. Minneapolis is too cold —about 46°—</u>
   <u>for water skiing in April.</u>

2. Los Angeles will hold a water skiing race in April.

   _____

   _____

3. Kids will make a snowman in Atlanta in October.

   _____

   _____

4. A baseball game in Atlanta will be rained out in July.

   _____

   _____

5. A baseball game in Seattle will be rained out in July.

   _____

   _____

6. Kids will have a snowball fight in Atlanta in January.

   _____

   _____

7. People need to use their air conditioners in Minneapolis in July.

   _____

   _____

8. People need to use their air conditioners in Los Angeles in October. _____

   _____

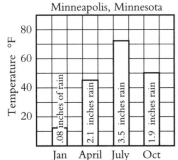

Minneapolis, Minnesota

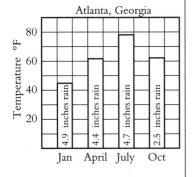

Atlanta, Georgia

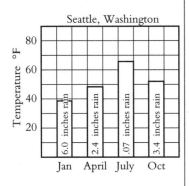

Seattle, Washington

NAME_____

The Winner, Water

Host: This year's Most Valuable Substance on Earth award goes to . . .
the envelope please. And the winner is . . . WATER!

Dr. Wett: On behalf of Water, I'd like to present this typical scene. It
shows the water cycle.

**Write (L) liquid, (G) gas, or (S) solid on the line to show
water's state at the start of each step in the water cycle.**

Liquid water
turns solid or
freezes at
temperatures
below 32°F.
Above 32°F,
water melts.
Particles of
liquid water
evaporate at any
temperature
above 32°F.
Water in the air
condenses, or
turns back to
liquid, when it is
cooled.

5. Water in the air condenses
to form a cloud_____

6. Condensed
water falls
as the rain

7. Frozen water
turns to snow_____

1. Snow
melts

4. Lake water
evaporates

2. Water runs down a stream _____

3. Water collects in
a lake _____

**Can you figure out what happens to water in each case?
Write *freeze, melt, condense,* or *evaporate* on the line.**

8. You leave a bottle outside overnight in the winter and it bursts. _____

9. Fog appears on the windshield of a car on a cool night. _____

10. A town near a mountain has a flood. _____

11. After reheating soup, you find there is less soup in your bowl. _____

NAME _____

Arky's Big Dig

Arkansas Smith sent all of the artifacts from his big dig to the World History Museum. Unfortunately, Elwood Fudge, Museum Director, lost all the labels. Using Arky's time line, help Fudge fix his foul-up, and label each box correctly.

Early Stone Age 20,000 B.C.
Crude chipped stone tools, wooden weapons, bow and arrow, sewing, cave painting, fire discovered 50,000 years earlier

Arky's time line shows you when things were widely used.

You're almost there! It's time to put this piece in place.

Middle Stone Age
8,000 B.C.–6,500 B.C.
Finely chipped stone tools, hand ax, chipped tools

Late Stone Age
6,500 B.C.–3,000 B.C.
Stone tools ground to a fine edge, domesticate animals, farming

Bronze Age
3,000 B.C.–1,000 B.C.
Sharp but brittle bronze weapons and tools, writing, bricks, horses, wheel, irrigation

Iron Age 1,000 B.C.–now
Superior iron tools and weapons

1. _____
   _____

| wood arrow |
| wagon wheel |
| bricks |
| broken bronze |
| spear |
| iron ore pebbles |

2. _____
   _____

| plow made of |
| bone |
| barrels of seeds |
| sharp ground |
| stone knife |
| charred firewood |

3. _____
   _____

| wood arrow |
| bone sewing |
| needle |
| charred firewood |
| crude stone hand |
| ax |

4. _____
   _____

| bricks |
| wagon wheels |
| iron plow |
| stone tablet with |
| writing |

5. _____
   _____

| chipped stone tool |
| wooden spear |
| animal skin sewn |
| together |
| metal clumps |
| flint stone knife |

NAME_____

Cracking the Code

Barb's new computer is on the fritz! Instead of printing the letter "B," it prints the letter "G." Instead of the letter "O," it prints the letter "U." Instead of the letter "R," it prints the letter "L." Translate Barb's letter to her friend Bob. Then write computer codes to fix the computer mistakes.

1. Write down what the letter should say on another piece of paper.

   DEAL GUG, THIS CUMPUTEL I GULLUWED FUL MY GUSINESS IS FLEAKING UUT! I'M VELY SULLY IF YUU CAN'T LEAD THIS. YUUL FLIEND, GALGALA

2. Use the computer map, or grid, for the letter "B" to write its computer code. Indicate whether each space should be black (B) or white (W). The code has been started for you.

1A-B	1B-___	1C-___	1D-___	1E-___	1F-___	1G-___	1H-___	1I-___
2A-W	2B-___	2C-___	2D-___	2E-___	2F-___	2G-___	2H-___	2I-___
3A-W	3B-___	3C-___	3D-___	3E-___	3F-___	3G-___	3H-___	3I-___
4A-W	4B-___	4C-___	4D-___	4E-___	4F-___	4G-___	4H-___	4I-___
5A-W	5B-___	5C-___	5D-___	5E-___	5F-___	5G-___	5H-___	5I-___
6A-W	6B-___	6C-___	6D-___	6E-___	6F-___	6G-___	6H-___	6I-___
7A-W	7B-___	7C-___	7D-___	7E-___	7F-___	7G-___	7H-___	7I-___
8A-W	8B-___	8C-___	8D-___	8E-___	8F-___	8G-___	8H-___	8I-___
9A-B	9B-___	9C-___	9D-___	9E-___	9F-___	9G-___	9H-___	9I-___

3. Make your own designs for the letters "O" and "R" above. Write a code that would tell a computer how to print each letter. Indicate which spaces should be white and which should be black.

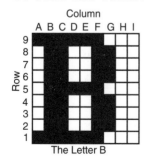

The Letter B

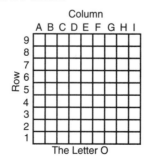

The Letter O

The Letter R

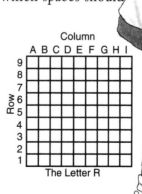

Grade 6

59

NAME _____

Be the Doctor

Good day, Doctor. Your job today is to treat patients with *diabetes* and *sickle-cell anemia*. Read through the patient histories. Then answer the questions.

Patient without Diabetes

1. The patient eats. Sugar from food enters the blood.
2. The pancreas releases insulin into the blood.
3. Insulin causes body cells to take sugar out of the blood.
4. The cells use the sugar for energy.

Patient with Diabetes

1. The patient eats. Sugar from food enters the blood.
2. The pancreas does not release enough insulin.
3. Sugar stays in the blood rather than going into the cells.

Put checks before the numbers to show which of the following symptoms could indicate that a patient has diabetes.

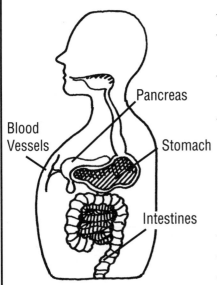

Blood Vessels

Pancreas

Stomach

Intestines

_____ 1. Symptom: The patient feels weak after eating.

_____ 2. Symptom: The patient's blood contains high levels of insulin.

_____ 3. Symptom: The patient's blood contains high levels of sugar.

_____ 4. Symptom: The patient's blood contains low levels of insulin.

Which of the following could be effective ways to treat diabetes? Put checks before the numbers. Explain your answers on the lines below.

_____ 5. Inject insulin into the blood.

_____ 6. Inject sugar into the blood.

_____ 7. Have the patient eat foods with lots of sugar.

_____

_____

_____

60

NAME

Patient without Sickle-Cell Anemia

1. Red blood cells carry oxygen (from the lungs) in the blood.
2. Red blood cells release oxygen to the body cells.

Normal red
blood cell

Patient with Sickle-Cell Anemia

1. Sickle shaped red blood cells clump together and clog small blood vessels.
2. The body removes the clogged cells.
3. The body now has a shortage of red blood cells.
4. Body cells become "starved" for oxygen.

Sickle-cell

Put checks before the numbers to show which symptoms you would look for in a patient that has sickle-cell anemia.

—— **8.** Symptom: The patient feels out of breath.
—— **9.** Symptom: The patient has sugar in his blood.
——**10.** Symptom: The patient's blood has clumped red blood cells.
——**11.** Symptom: The patient has relatives with sickle-cell anemia.

Which of the following could be effective ways to handle sickle-cell anemia? Put checks before the numbers. Use the space below to explain your answers.

——**12.** Have the patient avoid hard exercise.
——**13.** Have the patient eat foods that are red in color to get more red blood cells.

The *pancreas* is a gland that releases hormones and digestive chemicals. *Insulin* is a hormone that is sent to the body through the blood. *Sugar* is the fuel that cells use for energy. Without sugar, cells can't function.

Sickle-cell anemia is a genetic disease. This means that parents pass it on to children. But children don't get the disease unless they inherit the trait from both parents.

Plain Talk

Look at the chart. Read the information. Then circle the letter that best completes the sentences below.

	Tobacco	Alcohol	Marijuana	Cocaine and other illegal drugs
Legal/Illegal Age	legal for 18+	legal for 21+	illegal for all	illegal for all
Addictive	yes	can be	can be	yes
Number of abusers	60 million	11 million	8.2% of students 12–17	2.1 million
Method of use	smoke	drink	smoke	smoke, snort, inject
Effect	relaxes and stimulates	relaxes	mildly relaxes	stimulates or relaxes
Interferes with clear thinking	no	yes	yes	yes
Kills	from disease	from disease, from highway deaths, from overdose	from accidents and disease	from overdose, accidents, and disease
Diseases	cancer, heart and lung	liver and others	not yet known	not yet known
Yearly Deaths	400,000	200,000	less than 5,000	less than 5,000

1. The two most widely used drugs are
   A. tobacco and alcohol   **B.** tobacco and marijuana   **C.** alcohol and marijuana

2. An adult could be arrested for having
   A. tobacco   **B.** alcohol   **C.** marijuana

3. The drug that kills most people is
   A. cocaine   **B.** tobacco   **C.** alcohol

4. Traffic accidents can be caused by
   A. alcohol and cocaine   **B.** tobacco and marijuana   **C.** tobacco and alcohol

5. Smoking tobacco causes
   A. accidents   **B.** lung disease   **C.** confusion

6. It is illegal for people under 21 to
   A. drive a car   **B.** buy tobacco   **C.** buy alcohol

7. People die from overdoses of
   A. tobacco   **B.** cocaine   **C.** marijuana

NAME _____

Info About AIDS

What you know about AIDS could save your life. What you don't know could kill you. Write TRUE or FALSE for each of the statements below. Use reference materials to research your answers.

1. HIV is a virus that causes AIDS. _____

2. AIDS is a virus that causes HIV. _____

3. Viruses always cause disease. _____

4. The HIV virus lowers the body's ability to fight against infections. _____

5. In most cases, AIDS is passed from person to person through sex. _____

6. It is almost impossible to get AIDS without having sex or exchanging blood. _____

7. Safe sex will completely prevent AIDS. _____

8. Safe sex greatly lowers the probability of getting AIDS. _____

9. You can get AIDS by touching another person who has AIDS. _____

10. You can get AIDS by having contact with an infected person's blood or body fluids. _____

11. You can get AIDS from a blood transfusion. _____

12. You break out in a rash the day after you get AIDS. _____

13. The only way to find out if you have AIDS is to take a blood test. _____

14. You can have sex with an AIDS carrier without getting the disease. _____

15. Scientists have discovered a cure for AIDS. _____

16. Scientists have discovered drugs that are effective in fighting against AIDS. _____

17. The drugs that people take to fight AIDS are very expensive. _____

18. The only way to be safe from sexually transmitted AIDS is not to have sex at all. _____

To learn more about AIDS, contact one of these organizations: AIDS Education Project, 916-365-2304; Teens Tap, 800-234-TEEN.

It's time for the last puzzle piece. Cut it out and put it in place on page 64.

Puzzle

Here's where you glue or paste the puzzle pieces you cut out. When you put them all in place, you'll see your secret message.

64

Answers

Page 1
Graph should show:
Recommend Sparko Only: 1 dentist. Recommend Sparko and Other Toothpastes:
8 dentists.
Doesn't Recommend Sparko: 1 dentist.
1. Yes, 9 of 10 dentists recommended Sparko. But 8 recommendations were limited.
2. Zero of 10 thought Sparko was better than other toothpastes.
3. One dentist didn't recommend Sparko because it seemed too much like candy.

Conclusion: The recommendations were meaningless because most of the dentists didn't think Sparko was any better or worse than any other toothpaste.

Pages 2–3
1. Yes, the graph shows that points scored increases with height.
2. Answers will vary. Students should expect a 6-foot tall player to score 30 or more points per game.
3. No, the player with the most expensive sneakers did not score the most points. Similarly, the player with the least expensive sneakers did not score the fewest points.
4. There is no relationship between the cost of sneakers and number of points scored.
5. Answers will vary. There is no way to predict the number of points either player would score.
6. Yes, the more a player practices, the more points he or she scores.
7. Answers will vary. About 23 points per game.

Page 4
1. a. Answers will vary. Basic Burnt toast is the quickest recipe.
   b. Answers will vary. Burnt Toast Carbonara would seem to go well with spaghetti.
   c. Answers will vary. Scorchies would seem good for a party.
   d. Answers will vary. Midnight muffins might be good for a brunch.
2. Scorchies take 36 minutes longer to make.

3. 3 batches would take 3 x 22 = 66 minutes = 1 hr 6 minutes. 1 batch of Midnight Muffins takes 2 minutes longer.

Page 5
1. c
2. c

Plans for experiments will vary. Sample plans are given below.
Hot water freezes faster than cold water: Put hot and cold water in the freezer. Time how long it takes each to freeze.
Plants grow better when they listen to music: Play music in the room where one set of plants grow. Put identical plants in a second room with no music. Measure growth of each set of plants over the same period of time.
Eating junk food makes you "hyper". Look for behavorial changes after consuming junk food.

Page 6
Answers will vary. Sample Answers:
Hypothesis: Warm soda goes flat faster than cold soda.
Sample materials may include: plastic screw-top bottles of soda, plastic cups, freezer, hot water, clock.
Step 1: Warm one bottle of soda in hot water. Keep second bottle cold.
Step 2: Open both bottles. Pour an equal amount into two cups.
Step 3: Taste each sample after 5 minutes, 10 minutes, etc.

Page 7
Answers will vary. Sample Answers:
Warm soda goes flat faster than cold soda.
Procedure: 1. I needed one sample of warm soda and one sample of cold soda so placed one bottle of soda in hot water and put a second bottle in the refrigerator to keep it warm. 2. I poured an equal amount into two cups, making sure that the amount of soda in each cup didn't affect my results. 3. I tasted each sample every 5 minutes to see whether it had gone flat.

Results: Graph or table should reflect the amount of time it took for both the warm and cold soda to go flat.

1. Yes, warm soda went flat faster than cold soda.
2. The Bubble-Rageous Cola went flat so fast because it was warm. Warm soda goes flat faster than cold soda.
3. Gas escapes faster from warm soda than cold soda. This means that soda will go flat faster when it is warm than when it is cold.
4. The 100° soda. Gas escapes faster from warm liquid.

Page 8
1. A car gets and uses energy and responds to environmental changes.
2. A flame gets and uses energy, responds to environmental changes, and grows.
3. Bread mold gets and uses energy, responds to environmental changes, grows, reproduces, is made of cells, and is a living thing.
4. A light bulb gets and uses energy.

Page 9
1. **a.** green frog, garden spider
   b. African elephant
2. lungs, gills, body tubes
3. **a.** garden spider, African elephant
   b. green frog
4. African elephant

Page 10
1. sea anemone, lobster, fish, clam, jellyfish, starfish
2. butterfly, lobster, fish, clam, frog, lizard, sea gull
3. butterfly, sea anemone, lobster, clam, jellyfish, starfish
4. sea anemone, clam
5. clam

Page 11
Animal cards will vary.

Page 12
1. C-16 hours, D-16 hours, E-8 hours, F-12 hours
2. No, a lot of light or a little still could result in flowering.
3. Any plant that got 9 or more hours of darkness flowered.

4. Sample hypothesis: Any plant that gets more than 9 hours of darkness will flower.
5. Grow plants in different conditions. If you give them more than 9 hours of darkness you would expect them to flower.

Page 13
blobster—mitochondrion
glurk—cytoplasm
bagette—cell membrane
doo-hickey—nucleus
goo-goos—chromosomes
pouchie—nuclear membrane
blebs—ribosomes
sackette—vacuole
curly-Q—canal network

Page 14
1. 5 ft 6 $\frac{3}{4}$ in. She will reach her goal.
2. 6 ft 2 in.
3. He is likely to be 6 ft 4 in. rather than 6 ft 2 in.
4. Answers will vary.
5. Answers will vary.

Page 15
Writing: Answers will vary, but most students will see potential to improve their writing.
Blinking: Answers will vary. Students should conclude that they could not learn to avoid blinking completely.
Conclusion: Writing with your eyes closed is learned behavior, and blinking after a clap in your face is inborn behavior.

Page 16
1. Completely useless. The walls will not keep out heat or hold in cold.
2. Useful. The insulating walls will keep heat out.
3. Useful. The zogite will conduct heat well.
4. Useless. The gryb will not conduct heat well.
5. Fairly useless. Zogite soles will make the feet cold while gryb uppers will work fairly well.
6. Fairly useful. Porchgar soles will keep the feet warm while enkon uppers will work all right.

Page 17
1. When you bit the candy, you applied physical pressure or mechanical energy.

2. the sparks
3. It changed into electrical energy.
4. She was able to see her opponents because their candies created sparks.

Page 18
1. It was easier to move after the filled balloon was attached.
2. It reduced friction.
3. It is easier to slide on ice than on a rough floor because the ice reduces friction.

Page 19
2. early human
3. chimpanzee
4. modern human
5. early human
6. chimpanzee
7. modern human

Page 20
1. a. Dinosaur in Jurassic
   b. Amphibian in Permian
   c. Shark in Carboniferous
   d. Trilobites in Ordovician
   e. Jellyfish in Cambrian
2. D
3. B
4. Ordovician
5. about 390 million years ago

Pages 21–22
Answers will vary.

Page 23–24
Answers will vary.

Page 25
Energy to Go
Biological Energy, Solar Energy

Energy to See
Light Energy, Electrical Energy, Mechanical Energy, Solar Energy

Energy to Win
Mechanical Energy, Biological Energy, Chemical Energy, Solar Energy

Page 26
2. Pisces
3. $\frac{1}{2}$, Gemini
4. $\frac{3}{4}$, Virgo
5. Sagittarius would be in view. You'd know a year had passed because you'd be seeing the same constellations you saw 12 months or 365 days earlier.

Page 27
1. true
2. false
3. true
4. false
5. false
6. true
7. true
8. false
9. true
10. false
11. false
12. true

Page 28
Answers will vary.

Page 29
Sample Answers:
1. No sunblock; no water.
2. No life jackets; shouldn't swim after eating; shouldn't swim alone; shouldn't dive in shallow, rocky water; shouldn't swim near power boats.
3. Sledding without looking ahead; headed toward 3 young kids who are walking on the hill; ignoring unsafe ice; Jane and Bill wear no coats or hats; Jane shows no regard for younger kids.

Pages 30–31
1. Answers will vary.
2. Digestive, respiratory, and circulatory systems
3. The skeletal-muscular system.
4. Sample answers: Breathing problems, digestive problems, heartbeat problems, chemical release problems.
5. Answers will vary.

Page 32
Answers will vary.

Page 33

1. Evidence for: Interviews with dog owners, frisbee catching, command experiment, dog magazine article. Evidence against: Interviews with cat owners, mouse catching, cat experiment, cat magazine article.

2–5. Answers will vary.

Page 34

Bob Barski: Android
Jemma Urbb: Human
47-P5 Howard: Clone
Mary Jean Felkins: Robot

Page 35

1. Straight Green-Blue Rounder
2. Curly Blue-Green Boxie
3. Straight Blue-Green Roundie
4. Curly Green-Blue Boxer

Page 36

Answers will vary.

Page 37

Answers will vary.

Page 38

Nancy Heartthrob: Commensalism—Nancy is helped by her relationship to Johnny. Johnny is not affected either way.
Sid Porshay: Mutualism—Both Sid and Johnny benefit from the relationship.
Larry Foznik—Parasitism: Larry benefits from the relationship; Johnny is harmed by the relationship.
Jack Rabbit Records—Predation: Jack Rabbit consumes other companies.
Toni Thresh—Mutualism: Both Toni, Johnny, and Toni's students benefit from the relationship.
Jonnie Throbhart—Commensalism: Jonnie benefits greatly from the relationship; Johnny isn't harmed or helped.

Page 39

Answers will vary.

Pages 40–41
Largest Deserts
Asia—China
Desert Animals
Snakes
Mice
Desert Plants
Bushes
Vines

Largest Rainforests
South America—Brazil
Asia—Vietnam
Rainforest Animals
Monkeys
Tree frogs
Rainforest Plants
Orchids
Ferns

Largest Grasslands
African Savanna—Kenya
Central Asia—Russia
North America—Kansas
Grassland Animals
Antelope
Rabbits
Hawks
Grassland Plants
Grasses
Bushes
Flowering plants

Page 42

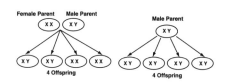

1. 0 males, 4 females.
2. 2 males and 2 females.
3. 0 females, 4 males.
4. Sexual reproduction.

Page 43

1. Water expands in volume when it freezes.
2. Water shrinks in volume when it melts.

3. Mark the height of frozen water, let the water melt, then mark the height of the melted water.
4. Hedda and Fredda should not send back their ice cubes. Refreezing will restore the cubes to their original size so they fill their cube cases.

Page 44
1. 52 grams
2. 64 grams
3. 48 grams
4. 16 grams
5. 216 grams

Page 45
1. Adding pebbles caused the cup to overflow. Adding sugar did not cause the cup to overflow.
2. The sugar dissolved in the water.
3. The sugar found gaps between water molecules, so when it dissolved, it didn't take up any extra space in the water solution. Evidence of this was the fact that the cup did not overflow.
4. When a material dissolves, it finds holes or gaps in the liquid in which it dissolves.

Page 46
1. They got faster as they heated up. You could tell because the warmer air made the spiral move.
2. To go higher, make the air in the balloon hotter; make it cooler to go lower.
3. mechanical energy

Page 47
1. The claim appeared to be correct.
2. You do not still see refraction because the bottle has been taken away. Apparently, going through the water is what changed the speed of the light and caused it to slow down.
3. Answers will vary.
4. Light changes speed and appears to bend when it goes through a medium other than air.
5. You might see refraction in light going through water, glass, plastic, or any other transparent medium.

Page 48
1. White or light grayish color
2. Diane was right.
3. red, orange, yellow, green, blue, and purple
4. If you left some of the colors out you would see a color other than white.

Pages 49–50
Experiment 1: The ball moves right when hit from the left and left when hit from the right.
Experiment 2: The ball doesn't move; it stays in place.

1. You are applying force by pushing on the Ball 1 with another ball.
2. left, right, above, below
3. The ball will move in the same direction in which the force that strikes it is traveling.
4. The ball won't move at all. The two forces cancel each other out.
5. In a diagonal direction up and to the left. It moves in a "northwest" direction, midway between straight up and straight left. Each force pushes the ball in the direction that it is traveling.
6. Answers will vary. Each force has its own effect on the object. The stronger the force, the more influence it has on the object's motion.
7. Answers will vary. Yes, pool balls move according to forces applied to them.

Page 51
1. It should balance.
2. It should balance only at the center of gravity. Students should conclude that the center of gravity is an object's balance point.
3. The shape will balance on its center of gravity.

Page 52
1. At the $\frac{1}{8}$ and $\frac{7}{8}$ positions. In degrees, at 45° and at 315°.
2. At the $\frac{1}{4}$ and $\frac{3}{4}$ positions. In degrees, at 90° and at 270°.
3. At the $\frac{1}{2}$ and original positions. In degrees, at 180° and at 0°.
4. At full moon and no moon (180° and at 0°). During those times, both the sun and moon are lined up.

Page 53
1. The gas pressure building up in the bottle.
2. Sample answer: The kitchen volcano might explode. A real volcano would also explode if it were sealed for too long.
3. Sample answer: They are different because real magma is liquid rock and cools to become igneous rock. Kitchen magma is mostly foam.

They are the same in the way they shoot out of the volcano.

Page 54
1. Sample answers: It is similar because it is made of sand layers that were pressed together and have an adhesive binding them. It is different because the adhesive is not natural and the layers were not laid down over millions of years.
2. There is more weight above the lower layers, which applies more pressure to the upper layers.
3. Sample answers: Students may mention different amounts of pressure, the type of sediment pressed together, and the stickiness of the adhesive that binds the layers together.

Pages 55–56
2. UNLIKELY. L.A. is cool but not cold in April.
3. UNLIKELY or HIGHLY UNLIKELY. The temperature is too warm to snow in October.
4. SOMEWHAT LIKELY. It rains 4.7 inches in July in Atlanta.
5. UNLIKELY. It rains 0.7 inches in July in Seattle.
6. UNLIKELY. The temperature is normally above freezing in January.
7. LIKELY. Minneapolis is hot during the summer.
8. UNLIKELY. The average temperature is not hot.

Page 57
1. solid
2. liquid
3. liquid
4. liquid
5. gas
6. liquid
7. solid
8. freeze
9. condense
10. melt
11. evaporate

Page 58
1. Bronze Age. The spear and wheel give it away. Iron ore pebbles do not show that iron is being used yet. The arrow originated much earlier and is still used.
2. Late Stone Age. The seeds show a farming community. The stone tools show that it is not yet the Bronze Age.
3. Early Stone Age. The crude stone ax clinches it for the Early Stone Age. Arrow, needle, and firewood were used in other eras as well.

4. Iron Age. All artifacts come from Bronze Age or later. The iron plow clinches it for the Iron Age.
5. Middle Stone Age. Metal clumps indicate that metal is not being used for tools yet. The flint knife, chipped tools, and sewn skins indicate the Middle Stone Age.

Page 59
1. Dear Bob, This computer I borrowed for my business is freaking out! I'm very sorry if you can't read this.
   Your friend, Barbara
3.

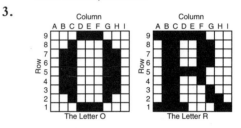

Pages 60–61
Check 1, 3, 4, 5
5. Injecting insulin into the blood might work because it would allow cells to take up sugar.
6. Injecting sugar into the blood wouldn't help because it still would not allow the cells to take up the sugar.
7. Eating foods with a lot of sugar would not help because there would be no way for the sugar to enter the cells without insulin.

Check 8, 10, 11, 12
12. This might help a person who lacked oxygen.
13. Red food would not increase the number of red blood cells.

Page 62
1. A
2. C
3. B
4. A
5. B
6. C
7. B

Page 63
1. True.
2. False.
3. False.
4. True.
5. True.
6. True.
7. False.
8. True.
9. False.
10. True.
11. True.
12. False.
13. True.
14. True.
15. False.
16. True.
17. True.
18. True.

How Do You Foster Your Child's Interest in Learning?

In preparing this series, we surveyed scores of parents on this key question. Here are some of the best suggestions:

- Take weekly trips to the library to take out books, and attend special library events.

- Have lots of books around the house, especially on topics of specific interest to children.

- Read out loud nightly.

- Take turns reading to each other.

- Subscribe to age-appropriate magazines.

- Point out articles of interest in the newspaper or a magazine.

- Tell each other stories.

- Encourage children to write journal entries and short stories.

- Ask them to write letters and make cards for special occasions.

- Discuss all the things you do together.

- Limit TV time.

- Watch selected programs on TV together, like learning/educational channels.

- Provide project workbooks purchased at teacher supply stores.

- Supply lots of arts and crafts materials and encourage children to be creative.

- Encourage children to express themselves in a variety of ways.

- Take science and nature walks.

- Teach children to play challenging games such as chess.

- Provide educational board games.

- Supply lots of educational and recreational computer games.

- Discuss what children are learning and doing on a daily basis.

- Invite classmates and other friends over to your house for team homework assignments.

- Keep the learning experiences fun for children.

- Help children with their homework and class assignments.

- Take trips to museums and museum classes.

- Visits cities of historical interest.

- Takes trips to the ocean and other fun outdoor locations (fishing at lakes, mountain hikes).

- Visit the aquarium and zoo.

- Cook, bake, and measure ingredients.

- Encourage children to participate in sports.

- Listen to music, attend concerts, and encourage children to take music lessons.

- Be positive about books, trips, and other daily experiences.

- Take family walks.

- Let children be part of the family decision-making process.

- Sit down together to eat and talk.

- Give a lot of praise and positive reinforcement for your child's efforts.

- Review child's homework that has been returned by the teacher.

- Encourage children to use resources such as the dictionary, encyclopedia, thesaurus, and atlas.

- Plant a vegetable garden outdoors or in pots in your kitchen.

- Make each child in your family feel he or she is special.

- Don't allow children to give up, especially when it comes to learning and dealing with challenges.

- Instill a love of language; it will expose your child to a richer thought bank.

- Tell your children stories that share, not necessarily teach a lesson.

- Communicate your personal processes with your children.

- Don't talk about what your child did not do. Put more interest on what your child did do. Accept where your child is at, and praise his or her efforts.

- Express an interest in children's activities and schoolwork.

- Limit TV viewing time at home and foster good viewing habits.

- Work on enlarging children's vocabulary.

- Emphasize learning accomplishments, no matter how small.

- Go at their own pace; People learn at different rates.

- Challenge children to take risks.

- Encourage them to do their best, not be the best.